Counseling
for Problems
of Self-Control

RESOURCES FOR
CHRISTIAN COUNSELING

RESOURCES FOR CHRISTIAN COUNSELING

(Other volumes forthcoming)

VOLUME ELEVEN

Counseling for Problems of Self-Control

RICHARD P. WALTERS, Ph.D.

RESOURCES FOR CHRISTIAN COUNSELING

General Editor

Gary R. Collins, Ph.D.

WORD PUBLISHING

Dallas · London · Sydney · Singapore

Library of Congress Cataloging-in-Publication Data:

Walters, Richard P., 1935–
  Counseling for problems of self-control.

  (Resources for Christian counseling ; v. 11)
  Bibliography: p.
  Includes index.
  1. Self-control—Religious aspects—Christianity.
2. Pastoral counseling. I. Title. II. Series.
BV4647.S39W35 1987   253.5   87-23122
ISBN 0-8499-0594-X

9 8 0 1 2 3 9 AGF 9 8 7 6 5 4 3 2

Printed in the United States of America

CONTENTS

EDITOR'S PREFACE

HAVE YOU EVER LOST YOUR TEMPER? Are there times when you overeat and put on weight? Does your schedule sometimes get so busy that your prayer life is crowded out? Do you ever find thoughts of lust, envy, anger, or jealousy swirling around in your mind?

Most of us, I suspect, would have to answer yes to all of these questions. Despite the many biblical injunctions about self-control, there are times when we all lose control and feel the guilt and frustration that follow.

For many people, including those who come for counseling, this is a serious problem. Compulsive drinkers, overeaters, shoplifters, gamblers, and smokers have problems with self-control. The same is true for people who gossip persistently, masturbate compulsively, periodically explode in violent anger or feast their eyes and minds on pornography. These actions may be followed by confession and a determination to stop the compulsive behavior, but too often this reform is short-lived.

Even while they talk with you in counseling, some of these people are thinking about repeating the actions that brought them into your office for help.

It is surprising that so few books deal with this issue, but in the pages that follow, Richard Walters gives a clear and insightful discussion of the causes and treatment of self-control problems. He introduces us to Bram whose uncontrolled violence at home scared his wife and caused her to call a counselor. We meet several other people who not only showed disorders of self-control but who were helped permanently by the biblically based and psychologically sound methods and counseling approach that the author describes in the pages that follow.

Dr. Walters has produced a volume that fits well into the Resources for Christian Counseling series. Each of these books is intended to deal with some topic that is likely to come up in your counseling. Written by counseling experts, each of whom has a strong Christian commitment and practical counseling experience, these volumes are intended to be examples of accurate psychology and careful use of Scripture. Each is intended to have a clear, evangelical perspective, careful documentation, a strong practical orientation, and freedom from the sweeping statements and undocumented rhetoric that sometimes characterize books in the counseling field. Our goal is to provide books that are clearly written, practical, up-to-date overviews of the issues faced by contemporary Christian counselors. All of the Resources for Christian Counseling books have similar bindings and together they will comprise a complete encyclopedia of Christian counseling.

In some way, most of the topics discussed in this series deal indirectly with a lack of self-control. This volume faces that issue directly. It begins by giving a detailed overview of self-control problems in general. Then we are given specific examples showing how the counseling principles can be applied. In your work, you probably will encounter self-control issues that are not discussed in these pages, but the author's general counseling principles give a format for dealing with new problems that may come into your counseling room.

I first met Richard Walters when we both were employed at a

Christian liberal arts college in St. Paul, Minnesota. Rich was a business administrator; I was a novice instructor in psychology. After several years we each left the school and Rich went on to take training that eventually led to a doctorate in psychology. Dr. Walters is a gentle man with a deep commitment to Christ, a strong involvement in the local church, a sensitivity to the needs of his family, unusual counseling skills, a delightful spark of humor, and an unusual understanding of people who struggle with anger, greed, lust, jealousy, and other problems of self-control. All of this comes out in the pages that follow.

The fascinating case histories, practical counseling guidelines, and useful materials to share with your counselees all make this an unusually helpful book. Best of all, the following pages are filled with references to the Word of God and to the Holy Spirit who alone give counselees and their counselors the ability to live Christ-honoring lives that are characterized by lasting self-control.

Gary R. Collins, Ph.D.
Kildeer, Illinois

INTRODUCTION

THE PIANIST CRIED OUT IN DESPAIR to the singer, "I play on the white notes and I play on the black notes—why must you sing in the cracks?"

Disorders of self-control fracture harmony among people. They are ugly, discordant conditions, with as many variations as notes on a piano, including the cracks.

Who would claim a full measure of self-control? Difficulty with self-control is universal. Most of us will quickly confess with Paul that we don't have the consistency we would like to have, yet we look down on people whose lives are disrupted by lack of self-control, probably because we recognize ourselves in them.

There is no clinical entity "disorder of self-control." In trying to define and catalog the problem area one would include dozens of entities. Some are pervasive: alcoholism, other drug abuse, eating disorders. Some are uncommon: pyromania, kleptomania. Some are dismissed as inconsequential by mental health professions but are brought frequently to Christian counselors who well know the devastation they can wreak: chronic lust, envy, shame, or perfectionism—to name a few.

A disorder of self-control creates problems, but at center it is a symptom of other problems. The most important task of this book is to show how you can help people identify and find resolution of the root problems from which their disorder grows. After identifying thirty different disorders I realized you wouldn't need all those descriptions. You will hear all you need from your counselees, whose experiences will be different than the typical anyway. We will concentrate on resolving the problems.

There is no quick fix for lack of self-control. Dramatic leaps of progress, intriguing turns of insight, and rapid closure of long-standing wounds are not uncommon, and offer thrilling counterpoint to the disappointment and drudgery that drag on when discontrolled persons reject change.

Because the disorders are often complex and deeply embedded in the person's lifestyle, and because the disordered person (or friends or family members) may resist counseling, it is a high calling to counsel a person with a self-control problem. Don't bother with it unless you enlist God's resources fully in the process.

Do we earn self-control or is it a gift from God? Scripture shows that both avenues are important. Some of the recent contributions of cognitive-behavioral psychology offer methods that can help us apply the Bible's injunctions to bring our house in order, but it is usually an exercise in futility to promote self-control without inviting the full participation of the Holy Spirit. Knowing what to do is easy; the empowerment of God's grace makes it possible.

I am grateful to Jim Waters for wise coaching; to Bob Rigdon for his innovative teaching; to the ebullient Gary Collins for encouragement, patience, high professional standards, and for exemplifying joy in Christ; to Ed McQueen, Roger Pitts, Brad Whitney, and the Tuesday morning and Wednesday evening groups for prayerful support and for holding my feet to the fire as Christian brothers ought; and to Rachel, Dan, and Amy for meaning more to me than I could describe on this page.

All Scripture in this volume is from the New International Version unless otherwise noted. Names of counselees have been changed in the interest of protecting the privacy of the individuals and their families.

Counseling
for Problems
of Self-Control

RESOURCES FOR
CHRISTIAN COUNSELING

PART I

FOUNDATIONS

CHAPTER ONE

A SURVEY OF THE PROBLEMS

"I'M SCARED. REALLY SCARED. It's my husband. He got mad last night, screaming and throwing things. Well, that's happened before, but this time he hit me. He said he'd kill me if I ever picked on him again, and I don't even know what I did."

Is it surprising that the woman was distressed? Her husband seemed out of control, showing what counselors might call the self-control disorder of explosiveness.

Examples of self-control disorders are common. "Our daughter-in-law called and we were just horrified. She says our son has been staying home from work drinking for the last two weeks and that he has gambled away their savings." Here we see two self-control disorders, alcohol abuse and pathological gambling.

"Pastor, my husband is spending money about twice as fast as he makes it. The bills are piling up and I'm getting threatening phone calls from the utility company, but he won't even listen to me. Last week he bought a motorcycle for $6,000 and . . . ." This is the self-control disorder of financial irresponsibility.

"I can't control my thoughts. Every time I look at a woman— *any* woman, *every* woman—I start thinking about sex with her. I'm ashamed, and I'm scared, but I can't stop it!" The man's self-control disorder is lust.

"My wife is hounding me constantly about where I've been, who I've been talking to, why I am three minutes late getting home. It's like living with the Gestapo. She's driving me out of the marriage." This is the self-control disorder of jealousy.

"She has gotten so strict with the children it breaks my heart. She doesn't let them watch a thing on TV. They can't eat a cookie anywhere in the house but the kitchen, and they must always be quiet. Always! Even when they are playing outdoors she will scold them if they yell! Don't you think she should let the kids be kids?" This is the self-control disorder of regimentation.

Unusual cases? I wish they were. But most pastors and counselors have heard problems like these many times. Each of these situations involves a failure in self-control. Although the problems may be less extreme, self-control can be a problem for all of us. The apostle Paul knew the difficulty of self-control. He said, "For what I do is not the good I want to do; no, the evil I do not want to do—this I keep on doing" (Rom. 7:19).

It does not surprise us that people seem to be more out of control than in control. We all have problems of self-control because our human condition is inclined toward evil. We love darkness rather than light (John 3:19). "All of us have become like one who is unclean, and all our righteous acts are like filthy rags; we all shrivel up like a leaf, and like the wind our sins sweep us away" (Isa. 64:6). (See also: Job 5:7; Isa. 53:6; Rom. 3:10, 23).

Humanists say that humans can be self-controlled if they use their strength and wisdom, but human effort is usually superficial and always riddled with harmful irregularities. It fails because "the wisdom of this world is foolishness in God's sight" (1 Cor. 3:19). Noting rampant disorders of self-control, pessimists assert that disorders of self-control are inevitable and hedonists define morality to accommodate them.

But self-control is possible. The Scriptures call for it, show how it can be attained, and relationship with God through Christ enables it!

WHAT IS SELF-CONTROL?

Self-control is managing our attitudes, feelings, and actions so they serve our long-term best interests and those of others. Self-control comes to people who learn discipline and social skills. It increases in those who accept God's grace in their lives and who seek to know and apply divine truth in a disciplined manner.

Self-control problems show great variation. Some problems, such as lustful thinking and envy, are individual and hidden. The effect on other persons is usually indirect and mild. Other problems, such as jealousy and impulsive overspending, are more visible and may affect family members quickly and radically. Alcoholism and compulsive gambling encompass a person's entire lifestyle. Still other problems, such as kleptomania and sexual perversions, are criminal offenses that create victims and may lead to arrest and confinement of the perpetrator.

SELF-CONTROL AND THE NEED FOR CHANGE

In addition to creating havoc in the lives of others, the person who lacks self-control is vulnerable to problems from without, "like a city whose walls are broken down" (Prov. 25:28). They may be condemned and rejected, lose their jobs, suffer from illness, and have severe financial problems. Without healing of the root conditions that find expression in disordered self-control, there will be new and more severe problems.

The person may have become so enmeshed in self-centered behavior that change seems almost impossible. Change will *not* begin until the person sees the benefits of self-control and desires to grow up and control his or her own thinking and behavior. This usually does not happen until they "hit bottom," when being out of control has become so painful that the process of change looks less painful than not changing.

Rebellion Is Common

Persons who have problems of self-control often know what to do but are unwilling to demand change from themselves. They rebel against truth and discipline offered from other persons just as they rebel against the truth and discipline they urge upon themselves.

The style of their rebellion may be congenial. Lewis, an alcoholic, tearfully pledged sobriety and expressed gratitude to his friend, Gerald, who had pled with him to stop drinking. Lewis admitted later that even as he was talking and praying with Gerald, he was planning how he would get his next drink.

The rebellion may be violent. Andy threw a chair through the picture window of his living room the night his wife asked him to go with her to a marriage counselor.

The rebellion may create extreme grief and fear. Suzi, age sixteen, ran away from home to escape consequences of her lack of self-control. For three years her parents did not know whether she was dead or alive.

The rebellion may be tragically self-defeating. Tony didn't want anything from life but pleasure. At college, he played arcade machines and pool until he flunked out. He moved into a house with five men and three women and used drugs to the point of permanent brain damage. He now lives in a halfway house, works in a sheltered workshop, and is dimly aware that his I.Q. once was near-genius.

The rebellion may sap the patience and compassion of family and friends. People who lack self-control often avoid counseling unless they see how it can be used to meet their childish goals, in which case their tactics are a challenge to even the most experienced counselors.

Simplistic Answers Aren't Enough

It is easy to say what these persons need: Christian maturity. But it is not easy to motivate them to pursue it. Sometimes counselors lose patience in the counseling process because change is so slow.

Self-control does not come easily to us, either. When we counsel with those who lack self-control it may be difficult to practice what we preach. As we counsel, we should examine ourselves to see if we are living at the level of maturity we commend to the client; we should recognize and repent of smugness or condemnation of the client. "'If any one of [us] is without sin, let him be the first to throw a stone . . . '" (John 8:3).

Disordered Persons Can Change

Nevertheless, people do change because of God's grace. The healing power of God's truth and presence, made more tangible and meaningful by your presence as counselor/friend, leads to change.

This book can help you be effective in counseling persons who have disorders of self-control. Part One describes principles and processes that apply to disorders of self-control generally. Chapters 1 and 2: practices of the problem; chapter 3: explanation of the problem; chapter 4: explanation of resolution; chapters 5–12: practices of resolution.

In Part Two, chapters 13–18 deal with specific problem areas and give more specific instruction on how to help people resolve root problems. Case studies show how the application of the counseling principles can apply to several kinds of disorders.

The message of Part Three goes beyond counseling. While we can grow in self-control by using the human characteristics God has created in us, sufficient self-control comes only by putting control of our lives into his hands. Chapters 19 and 20 offer the biblical basis and process for growth in Christian maturity. This material is important in our own lives as well as for our clients.

None of the people who come to you will have histories exactly like the people in this book; your counselees will not react or talk like the people in the case studies. Therefore, the general principles and counseling processes outlined in the following pages may be more valuable to you than the specific case histories.

This book discusses a diverse group of disorders. I hope you never see them all the same week, but I hope also that persons with these conditions will find you. They need the help you can give. As you use your judgment and the counsel of the Holy Spirit to help them, you will see burdens lifted.

To the extent that Jesus Christ is the Lord of our lives, to that extent we see wonderful things happen in the lives of those whom God brings to us for counsel. Let us pray as David, "May the words of my mouth and the meditation of my heart be pleasing in your sight, O Lord, my Rock and my Redeemer" (Ps. 19:14).

CHAPTER TWO

AN ILLUSTRATION OF THE PROBLEM

BRAM WILNOCK, 44, IS THE MANAGER of the parts department for an automobile dealer. He attends church regularly but is not a member. His wife Glenda is a vivacious woman who is involved in many church activities. They have three teenage children.

Bram periodically "explodes" in anger. This has happened about five times a year throughout the marriage. On these occasions he has shouted and cursed at Glenda or the children, and several times has thrown or broken things.

For several years Glenda encouraged Bram to have counseling. He reacted to each suggestion with tight-lipped silence and it was only after an evening of violence when Glenda called their pastor to their home that Bram reluctantly agreed.

Bram's beliefs and experiences illustrate eight elements involved in disorders of self-control. Here is a summary of information about Bram gathered during many counseling sessions.

1. *Needs: People do what they do because they want to fulfill needs.* Bram needs to be in harmony with the environment: physically comfortable and safe. He needs to be in harmony with other humans: to love and be loved. He needs to be in harmony with himself: to enjoy being Bram Wilnock and using his abilities. And he needs to be in harmony with God: to personally know and enjoy his Creator.

Needs are a result of Creation and the Fall. At Creation, humans were in perfect harmony with God, the environment, with one another, and within themselves as beings. This was disrupted by the Fall. Humans yearn for restoration from their fallen condition into harmony with God's lovingly designed order.

Bram's difficulties are not the result of faulty needs. His needs are normal, the same as yours and mine. Problems arise when he uses faulty methods to seek fulfillment or is blocked from adequate fulfillment. If we are to help Bram we must understand what needs are unfulfilled and why he uses methods that create more problems than they resolve.

2. *Root problems: Self-control problems often arise early in life.* The need for harmony in four areas of life was important to Bram when he was a child. Although he didn't know about them, he was striving to fulfill them. Learning about Bram's early life will help us understand why he lives as he does now.

Bram's father was a closet alcoholic whose behavior was unpredictable. Much of the time he was sarcastic and belittling, sometimes violent and physically abusive. His punishment of Bram usually was excessive. Bram's mother lived in fear of her husband and tried to protect herself from his wrath by anticipating what he would want and providing it before he asked. The need for harmony with the environment (physical safety) was not met in the home or neighborhood.

Bram, physically small for his age until late adolescence, was harassed by other boys throughout his school years. It was a very unhappy time for him and during the early stages of counseling he had few memories of his life before age ten.

His recollections from age ten through eighteen were painful, filled with incidents of being ridiculed and rejected at school and at home. During high school he got drunk most weekends. His need for harmony with others was not met. Rejection from his father and ridicule from peers marred the development of harmony with self, and he had no chance to learn about God and find harmony with him.

3. *Motivation: Unfulfilled needs, like an itch we want to scratch, lead people to action.* The difficult conditions during childhood left Bram incomplete and wounded. Now, in adult life, he can adequately fulfill some of his needs, but not others.

The Wilnocks have managed their income wisely over the years. Their needs for harmony with the environment (housing, financial security, physical protection) are adequately fulfilled. But Bram is not effective in fulfilling some other needs. He has little self-confidence in new social situations and in his roles as husband and father. In superficial social situations, such as at his American Legion meetings or with his bowling team, he is affable, but he talks to no one about his "heavy-duty" worries. His closest friend is the man who works for him but they do not talk about personal concerns. His need for harmony with others is not fulfilled.

Harmony with himself is low, which is not surprising since his self-concept was never nurtured at home or at school. There is "an empty place" in his life where the benefits of parental nurture and companionship should be. The harsh ridicule and rejection during childhood continue to "stab" him. This is the most important cause of his difficulties now. He has greatest self-confidence at work.

Harmony with God is low. Having never confessed and repented before God, he remains guilty. Although he believes in God, he views him as stern and unapproachable. Bram wishes he were sure that God would never notice him.

These conditions will begin to improve when Bram is taught by a compassionate counselor, but that will not be enough. Adequate resolution must include God's intervention. Bram's guilt will be remedied by God's forgiveness, "empty places" filled by God's presence, and resentment toward those who have wounded him will be released when he accepts God's

23

help in forgiving and living with new thinking. That has not happened yet.

4. *Defective systems: Sinful nature and limited understanding of life lead people to behavior that does not work very well.* Bram has had difficulty fulfilling his needs all his life because his systems for seeking fulfillment are defective. Let's see why.

First, he has that birth defect we all share—sinful nature. This, of course, leads him to harmful choices.

Then, his parents were not able to help him learn how to fulfill his needs. To the contrary, he developed many incorrect and unhealthy beliefs and attitudes. Although he did the best he could to cope with life within and outside the family, he did not have the information and skills he needed.

His many emotional wounds generated anger and fear. With anger, his autonomic nervous system (a portion of the total system) would quickly trigger a strong "fight/flight" reaction. (The physical changes that occur with anger or fear are familiar to us all. In Bram, they are unusually powerful.) Not knowing how to express his anger without getting in more trouble, and not knowing how to resolve the conditions that led to the anger, he swallowed his strong feelings of hurt, fear, loneliness, and worthlessness.

In response to the rejection he had as a child he began to believe such things as: "People will hurt me. People won't like me if they find out how I have behaved. People can't be trusted. Because my father rejected me, other people will too." He was not aware of these beliefs, but they influenced his behavior nonetheless.

Believing he was not worthwhile, he was dependent upon others for reassurance of his worth. He drew that from their praise or, more often, from the absence of the condemnation he expected from them.

During school years he avoided people because he got hurt part of the time when he was with them. He felt so unloved at home and in his hometown that he joined the navy to get away. There, men were leery of his quick temper and he was not hassled. He got some admiration off-duty for his drinking. He served as a supply clerk for four years, was fairly comfortable, and wishes now that he had stayed in the navy as a career.

He feared condemnation from authority figures. His method of coping with that fear was to keep a low profile. In grade school classes he was the quiet child who passed with minimal grades but never created a problem for the teacher. This style remains. He explains, "I get along well on my job because I give the boss everything he wants, and more. Of course if I didn't, no telling what would happen!"

Fear has always encompassed a large part of his life. He is often anxious without knowing why. He will not talk about that. Fear extends to God, whom Bram regards as an authority figure of great power and a vengeful nature. "I believe in him, but I don't know him very well. I have a hard time with the idea that he cares about me."

Bram's first experience in receiving praise for his work was in the navy. Since then he has worked hard to be accurate, complete, and to do more than is expected of him. That's good, but he doesn't assert himself for what he needs. For example, he has one helper in the parts department and knows he needs two, but he chooses to work under pressure rather than "make waves" (his words). He believes that if he asks for help "the boss will think I'm not cutting it and replace me." He worries that as he gets older he "may not be able to stay on top of it all" and lose his job. This shows a strong connection in his mind between his performance and his self-worth.

Because he believes that others tolerate him only because he performs to their satisfaction and that they would not like him if they knew the truth about him, he believes his worth is always in jeopardy. He is often uneasy about this. His tolerance for frustration is very low, but there are a lot of frustrating circumstances at home and at work. Since he doesn't talk about these things with anyone, he does not learn how to eliminate them or cope with them and he does not know how much affection and support others have for him.

Thus, pressure builds up until he explodes in anger. On these occasions he shouts and may throw or break something, or hit a wall or the floor with his fist. He has never struck a person.

Bram has done what has seemed best to him. He says, "I just want to be a good father and a good citizen. I don't think anybody owes me the world on a silver platter. I'm willing to work hard and do my part and that is what I have always tried to do—to do what is right in my own little place in the world."

He has self-control in some parts of life but not in others. As he seeks to fulfill the yearnings of his heart, he makes some damaging choices: he is passive when it would be proper to be assertive, he holds in feelings and concerns that need to be shared, and he has angry outbursts to get relief from the internal pressures. His family knows only about the outbursts. As counselor, you would learn about his defective systems and try to help him substitute effective thinking and behavior.

5. *Payoffs: Defective fulfillment systems produce some temporary benefits.* For Bram there is less pain in keeping his anger in (as long as he can) than in the fear of rejection if he tells someone about it. The outbursts also give him some fleeting payoffs (that seems to him to be beneficial). They release his pressure and give him a sense of being in control. Perhaps surprising to us, he feels most in control during his outbursts (when he appears to us to be completely out of control). This is because during those moments he is, at last, doing what he chooses to do instead of doing what he believes he must do in order to please others.

6. *Costs: Defective fulfillment systems produce some severe costs.* It is hard for him to swallow his fear and anger, and there are great costs associated with his explosive tantrums. They frighten his wife and children and alienate him from them. He feels guilty and ashamed. And the outbursts increase his fear that (a) he may be physically violent and (b) other persons will find out about his behavior and reject him because of it.

7. *Repetitions: When a system has some payoffs, people are likely to do it again.* Bram's system is: lack of fulfillment, frustration, belief that he will be rejected if he talks about his frustration with another person, decision to stifle the painful feelings, "toughing it out" as long as he can, exploding. He has been through this cycle many times.

The chain of events that led to Bram's disorder of self-control seemed orderly and logical to Bram as he went through it. As is true of most people, he did not see this as a progression, but took one event at a time without understanding the connections. The decisions he made, including destructive ones, seemed to him to be logical and sensible. You or I, looking from different perspectives, could have seen the fallacies of logic and predicted the problems that would arise; Bram could not.

8. *Disorder of self-control: What begin as normal responses will, when repeated, become so harmful they disrupt living.* Bram struggles with fear and shame every hour he is awake; he is in conflict with Glenda, and she and the children are afraid of and afraid for Bram. He is having difficulty at work and pulling away from friends. The tension is creating physical problems. These are conditions that mark the difference between ordinary life stress that will work out as time goes by and a disorder that needs and deserves the support, teaching, and confrontation of a counselor.

Summary. Bram and you and I have much in common: needs that motivate us, a nature born in sin, imperfect childhoods, striving to do what makes sense to us, and occasional use of defective systems for need fulfillment. Chapters 3 and 4 describe how problems of self-control begin and are resolved. These are written in general terms so you can apply the principles to people you work with but we will also follow Bram, so we can learn how the principles worked in his life.

CHAPTER THREE

THE BEGINNINGS OF THE PROBLEM

IN BRAM'S HISTORY WE SAW EIGHT ELEMENTS that are present in disorders of self-control. We shall now define each, describe its origin, and offer a summary of how each destructive element may be reversed. This will follow the chronological development of a self-control disorder. (The counselor usually learns about the client in the reverse sequence, learning about the client's recent history first and childhood later, so we will follow that order in the next chapter.) This developmental sequence is summarized on pages 30, 31.

BASIC HUMAN NEEDS

Every system of counseling rests on assumptions about the nature of human life. These assumptions must answer such

questions as: What is good for people? Why do people sometimes do things that are not good for them? How can people
change? How can one person help another?

Stated briefly, my assumptions include the belief that at the
time of creation humans were complete and in harmony with
God, the environment, other persons, and within themselves as
beings. Then Adam and Eve yielded to the temptation of Satan
(Gen. 3:1–13), who is God's enemy and the author of untruth.
Evil was introduced into the world (Gen. 3:14–24), the root
of the corruption we know today (2 Cor.; 2 Thess. 2:9, 10; 1
Pet. 5:8).

Human beings were created in the image of God (Gen. 1:26,
27), but God is so much more than us that the difference is
incomprehensible (1 Kings 8:27; Ps. 147:5). Within our limited
understanding, however, we see in God's nature characteristics
that we also find in human beings: capacities for knowledge,
unity, dominion, relationship, and righteousness.

God is all knowing (Ps. 147:4, 5; Prov. 3:19; Dan. 2:20, 21;
Rom. 11:33, 34). He is unified and complete (1 Kings 8:60;
Deut. 32:4; 1 John 1:5). God, Creator and owner of the universe, has dominion as its master (Gen. 1, 2; 18:14; Ps. 107:25,
29; 114:7, 8; 135:6; Matt. 19:26).

God is relational, as shown by his act of creating humans
(Isa. 43:1–15), his accessibility to us (Ps. 145:18; Rom. 5:2;
Eph. 2:13), and his love for us (John 3:16; Rom. 5:8). God is
holy, perfect in righteousness (Lev. 19:2; Ps. 18:30; 145:17;
Isa. 51:8; Matt. 19:17).

God is infinitely more than a human being, but even with
our limited understanding we can find in humans the imprint
of God's nature. Our needs, part of God's design of the human
condition, are dim, tiny, incomplete reflections of the nature
of God.

Before the Fall, Adam and Eve had everything they needed.
We still need what they needed before the Fall, but now we
must contend with obstacles and deficits that did not exist
before. For example, in relating to the environment we now
encounter disease, weeds, and ignorance. In our contacts with
other persons there is hostility, suspicion, and alienation. Within ourselves, there is sin, two-mindedness, and lack of insight.

29

Elements in the Development
of Self-Control Disorders

1. NEEDS Harmony with environment, other persons, self, God.
   Source: Creation. God designed the universe as harmonious.
   Resolution: fulfillment

2. ROOT PROBLEMS
   a. *Sinful human nature*
      Source: the Fall. We are all in rebellion with God at birth.
      Resolution: salvation
   b. *Physiological influences*
      Source: condition at birth, disease, accident. These, and the root problems below, are consequences of the Fall.
      Resolution: cope, overcome
   c. *Deficits from the past*
      Source: neglect by others. The failure of parents to nurture leads to defective systems for fulfillment.
      Resolution: forgive, receive healing
   d. *Wounds from the past*
      Source: actions of others. Physical or psychological abuse lead to distortions in need fulfillment systems.
      Resolution: forgive, receive healing
   e. *Discrepancies between one belief or part of life and another*
      Source: learned. When disharmony exists within an individual, proper harmony with God and the world is not possible.
      Resolution: relearned
   f. *The results of personal sin*
      Source: inevitable results of bad choices. Sins always carry penalties.
      Resolution: e.g., for shame to receive and accept God's forgiveness, or for physical consequences to learn to cope and overcome

3. MOTIVATION FROM UNFULFILLED NEEDS
   Source: natural order. The world, flawed by sin, does not`fulfill persons' needs.
   Resolution: understand and follow God's order for living

4. DEFECTIVE SYSTEMS FOR NEED FULFILLMENT
   Source: learned. Everybody tries to fulfill needs, but at times we all fail in the way we do it.
   Resolution: relearn, resist

5. PAYOFFS The attempts to fulfill needs produce payoffs (which may have constructive or destructive outcomes).
   Source: natural order
   Resolution: understand

6. COSTS
   Source: The inevitable consequences of using faulty patterns of need fulfillment.
   Resolution: understand

7. REPETITIONS
   Source: defective systems are repeated when
   a. the payoffs (whether real or illusory) outweigh the costs,
   b. the person does not know an alternative,
   c. the person is in physical or emotional addiction (bondage to sin).
   Resolution: detoxification, break habits

8. DISORDER OF SELF-CONTROL The faulty pattern is a disorder if it is repeated when costs outweigh payoffs.
   Source: chosen
   Resolution: all of the resolutions above, as part of the Isaiah 6:10 process

In our relationship with God we have guilt and mistrust; we cheat and finagle.

Human beings yearn to be restored to the completeness and harmony that existed before the Fall. They seek to restore the completeness and harmony that were there before. The yearning is best understood as four categories of need that motivate our thinking and behavior. Secular theorists have observed these, but have tended to focus on only one or two and ignore the compelling human desire to know our Creator. Therefore, their explanations of the problems are incomplete and their solutions inadequate. As we have seen, the four are:

1. *Harmony with the environment.* Humans need to pursue physical preservation and a sense of safety and security. When people are striving for self-preservation, responding to their biological urges, we see most clearly their similarity to ordinary animals. The works of Freud,[1] and of Skinner,[2] of Dollard and Miller,[3] and other behaviorists, emphasize this aspect of man's motivation.

2. *Harmony with other humans.* Incomplete without human partnership (as God affirmed in his creation of Eve, Gen. 2:15–23), humans need to love and to be loved; to belong to a community of other humans. Genesis 2:23, 24 institutes the family as the building block of society. We see development of community in the instructions in the Old Testament, emphasis on marriage and family throughout the Bible, and the importance of relationship as a body of believers in the New Testament.

Many students of human behavior have emphasized social gregariousness—human longing for affiliation and community, for caring about and being cared about by others. This is spoken to with emphasis in the writings of Sullivan,[4] Horney,[5] Fromm,[6] Berne,[7] and Adler.[8]

3. *Harmony with oneself.* Humans are, by nature, fragmented. Scripture speaks of the divided heart (Ezek. 11:19; Eph. 4:16–19). We need to find meaning and satisfaction, to be able to respect and love our own being, to fulfill the potential we have as creative beings. We seek the contentment promised in Scripture (Phil. 4:11; 1 Tim. 6:6).

Through the ages humans have consistently worked to better their condition. Much human labor can be explained in no other way than that it finds an inherent delight in self-improvement, in acts of altruism, and in the rewards of experiencing truth and beauty. This aspect of human motivation is described by Maslow,[9] who used the term "self-actualization" to identify this urge, and by Frankl in his astute observations of the role of meaning in life.[10] When Carl Rogers wrote "the organism has one basic tendency and striving—to actualize, maintain, and enhance the experiencing organism"[11] and when he described the drive toward congruence between self and ideal self, he emphasized portions of biblical truth about humans.

4. *Harmony with God.* In all cultures throughout history people have sought peace with God (Matt. 13:17). This longing is expressed poetically in many of the Psalms. See, for example, Psalms 42 or 84. This is our most important need, the only *essential* need. Secular theorists and researchers fail us and themselves when they attempt to use science to investigate and instruct us in this area, which science cannot reach. Let us not fail our counselees by failing to give careful and enthusiastic attention to this need; but let us not ignore the others either.

We saw how these four needs motivated Bram. You will observe that they motivate you and everyone else. Because needs originate as part of God's creation it is proper for us to seek fulfillment. Secular sources have not equipped people to do so with success, failing to instruct about God and encouraging people to use means of fulfillment that lead to spiritual, social, or biological problems.

In counseling we meet clients who have not known how to fulfill needs and who should be taught those life skills. Others have been blocked by root problems that need to be resolved. And others have not recognized that, while needs are morally neutral, the means of seeking fulfillment may be right or wrong, and they have tried to fulfill needs through sinful means. Part of counseling is giving education in the life skills of need fulfillment.

ROOT PROBLEMS

God created us with needs and designed us to seek their fulfillment, but no one's needs are fully met. Some of our problems arise when we try to fulfill our needs in ways that are contrary to God's design. Other problems result from sins of other persons whose actions interfere with the fulfillment of our needs.

Self-control problems are usually secondary problems, not the root problem. Bram joined the American Legion and a bowling team to help fulfill his need to be liked. This didn't work out because he remained emotionally aloof, a result of his root problem of mistrust. When root problems are resolved, secondary (self-control) problems are resolved relatively easily.

I propose that six root problems lead to most disorders of self-control. Each root problem is a manifestation of sin—an expression of the brokenness of our world. God, who is love, offers life-bringing alternatives to each. I will define them and, further in the book, show how you can help people find resolution and growth.

1. *Sinful nature.* The fundamental problem is sin, of course. Sin is rejection of God and is our natural condition because of the Fall. The person who has not accepted God's offer of salvation, relationship with him, will have one or both of two reactions. The first is pride. The urge rises within us, as it did in Lucifer, Adam, and Eve, to put ourselves above God. This leads to self-control disorders of gratification.

The second response style is fear. We recognize God's awesome authority but know only his wrathful nature. Living in fear of him we may also seek self-gratification, in this case not so much for the pleasure but to numb the pain. Fear leads to self-control disorders of escape.

God loved us as he designed us; we're created in such a way that if we live by his design, life will be meaningful. If our beliefs or actions go against God's design, we reap destruction. If we do not know God (even though a result of ignorance) we do not draw on God's healing power nor learn how to defend against injustice, cope with frustration, and avoid the traps of untruth.

Sinful human nature is the result of the Fall. It affects all of us, and the only valid response is to accept God's offer of salvation and to live in relationship with him.

2. *Physiological influences.* Biological characteristics influence how a person responds to life. This includes neurological

dysfunctions that may arise at birth, through accident, or as a by-product of other physical problems. For example, an intellectually disadvantaged child is frustrated at school while a child gifted with quickness to learn enjoys it. Someone like Bram, who has a quick, powerful, physical response when angry has an additional obstacle to maturity. Physical impairments may invite rejection and add frustration. Many people are predisposed by their physiology to depression, thought disorder, or chemical addiction.

Conditions that arise at birth or by accident are not volitional but our responses to them are volitional. Those conditions that make life more difficult are part of the curse upon the world that results from the Fall. Sometimes God removes such difficulties by healing through supernatural means. God *always* heals *life,* and it has seemed to me that his more common pattern is to bring people into joy and contentment by helping them cope and overcome.

The world is intrinsically cantankerous; there is built-in opposition to life and health. We see that in the other four root problems.

3. *Deficits* are parts of life that remain incomplete because certain positive experiences or relationships did not exist during childhood or adolescence.[12] For example, a junior-high-age boy needs to know that his father loves him. If there is no relationship (instead of a reassuring one) an emptiness exists. To cope with this deficit of reassurance the boy may seek a substitute source, perhaps membership in a gang. This will not be sufficiently fulfilling, so a deficit of reassurance continues. Bram's father rejected him, creating mistrust of people, especially authority figures. Deficits of parental nurture often remain the primary motivating force in persons' lives for years.

Deficits are resolved by forgiving the person who has sinned against us, receiving God's healing of the lingering effects, and living appropriately in relationship with those who are unhealthy toward us.

4. *Wounds* result from harmful events or attitudes expressed by parents or other persons. Ridicule or other rejection from peers, sexual abuse, harsh punishment or other physical abuse,

and unattainable expectations are just a few ways persons are wounded early in life.

No one has perfect parents. Even if one did he or she would have an oddball neighbor or relative who would mess up the parents' perfect work! For example, Bram was picked on by children at his school. This angered him but he was powerless to stop it. Feelings that came from these early experiences—anger, fear, disgust toward himself—carried over into adult life.

The only way to get rid of wounds is to forgive the person who caused them. We can't forgive without God's grace. The unsettling memories of traumatic events may be healed. When the offender does not offer restitution or effort toward reconciliation, the wounded person may need to learn charity and assertiveness.

5. *Discrepancies.* A discrepancy is a difference between two things. It is an inconsistency, a conflict between one part of life and another part. Discrepancies may be between:

Belief and God's truth
Belief and behavior
Behavior now and behavior earlier (or later)
Behavior and the rights of others
Beliefs or desires and social realities
Behavior and social realities

Discrepancies always generate emotional or mental stress. Discrepancies create problems even when both parts are valid. For example, a high school student wants to save money for college but uses two thousand dollars to go on a summer mission project. The two desires, both commendable, are in conflict. Discrepancies like this are as destructive to nonbelievers as to Christians.

Discrepancies are learned. Many of them rise from distorted beliefs. Beliefs about life are formed early and they influence development of personality and relational style. Among the most important beliefs are those that pertain to the basic needs: beliefs about the nature of God and morality and the world, the meaning of life, the role of relationships, and one's abilities and worth.

Beliefs are first shaped by experiences with other persons. A child whose mother is warm and tender when holding and touching him or her during the early days of life begins to develop trust in other people. Later, the child learns in other ways, such as listening to the beliefs of people near by. The child may learn, for example, that a loving God exists and that we may know him personally and receive his comfort and direction. Or the child may hear, and believe, that God is vindictive (as did Bram), indifferent, or that there is no God.

It is relatively easy to understand what a person wants, because there are only a few different needs. It is much more difficult to understand why people choose their particular pattern of need fulfillment because there are millions of patterns. Yet that is an essential part of the counseling task.

To understand people's activity patterns, we must understand their beliefs. Usually, the most time-consuming and important part of counseling is helping the client identify and change erroneous beliefs.

Distorted beliefs can generate painful emotions, such as fear, sorrow, or shame. They complicate many spiritual, emotional, and relational problems. Jesus describes the frantic pursuit of security and pleasure by those who follow the distorted beliefs the world teaches (Luke 12:16–34). The world's system is bogus (1 Cor. 3:19) and leads to compulsive disorders of self-control and other problems. By contrast, we can have quiet confidence when we aellow Christ's teaching, "But seek his kingdom, and these things will be given to you as well" (Luke 12:31).

Discrepancies are learned. What has been learned can be unlearned. The counselor may instruct about how to break habits, how to think logically, how to displace untruth with truth, and other mechanisms of living in harmony with God's moral order.

6. *Consequences of sins.* These are the inevitable results of bad choices, of behavior and attitudes that are wrong. Disorders create disorders. Witness the drug abuser who steals to support his habit or the alcoholic who loses her job. In the absence of God's grace, sins can only multiply. Consequences of sins may remain after conversion: the damaged liver of an alcoholic, damaged brain tissue of a drug abuser, or the indebtedness of a compulsive spender.

A person may develop a disorder by responding improperly to these residual conditions from earlier sins. The root problem in such a case is not just the earlier sin, but the failure to deal constructively with the subsequent conditions. Some of these consequences may be reversed. For example, the consequence of bankruptcy from impulsive spending may be remedied through diligent work and astute budgeting. On the other hand, the arm mangled and amputated as a result of an accident while drunk is not restored.

Counseling has sometimes given attention just to the disruptive behavior. "If he would only quit drinking, everything would be okay." But we must go beyond managing or even stopping the symptoms. The counselor must help the person dig down to the root problems from which the symptoms grow. Christian counseling leads the client to God's mercy and grace for the thorough cleansing and restructuring that result in effective living.

MOTIVATION FROM UNFULFILLED NEEDS

If people don't get their needs fulfilled they will be at least somewhat dissatisfied. Their "emotional bank account" will be impoverished. That's a hard way to live, so they try to have their needs met.[13]

If they can succeed in having a need partially met, they will accept that. If a need can be temporarily met, even at the price of a high cost later (for example, intoxication tonight, hangover tomorrow), they may go for it. Many do. This "play now, pay later" lifestyle is costly and shortsighted, but popular. It is a hard way to live.

Unfulfilled needs are part of healthy life because fulfillment never lasts. The need for relationship is satisfied but then a friend moves away. Financial security can be jeopardized by unemployment, or the boat of faith in God is torpedoed by the un-Christian behavior of one's pastor. These call for new initiatives—constructive thinking, action, worship, and praise. Because we live in an imperfect world, life requires these initiatives on a continuing basis.

The need is God's creation and is not a problem, but the manner of fulfillment may be. Denying that needs exist or that it is legitimate to seek fulfillment of them may become a problem (particularly among some legalistic Christian groups). The correctives are to understand God's design for human living and to learn effective ways of fulfilling needs. Christians have collective responsibility to remove obstacles to need fulfillment (such as racial discrimination, for example).

DEFECTIVE SYSTEMS FOR NEED FULFILLMENT

We all find ways to satisfy our needs and relieve discomfort. There are as many ways to do this as there are people. Some methods work, and many of them do not.

Disorders of self-control often come to people who don't know how to meet their needs. The principles and methods in this book will help you understand persons who use defective systems to meet their needs. Such an understanding will guide as you help them resolve their disorder and grow in Christian maturity.

Defective systems start early. When normal needs of childhood are not provided, a child tries various systems of behavior in an effort to fulfill needs. Children choose different systems.

The effectiveness of the system depends on what the child has learned from family or other people. If the child has been fortunate to learn a lot of truth, the system may work. Those whose beliefs are distorted or who lack information about how society works, are likely to choose behavior systems that don't work. This is common, and often leads to a disorder of self-control.

Often Bram stifles his feelings because he thinks people might reject him if they know how he feels. This works temporarily, but emotional pressure builds up until he explodes in rage to relieve it. This is a defective system for coping with his feelings.

Defective systems are learned. Resolution comes by breaking the cycle and displacing the defective system with God's system.

PAYOFFS FROM DEFECTIVE FULFILLMENT SYSTEMS

The person who is "out of control" chooses a system for fulfillment expecting to benefit from it. Rightly so. Every system, including those that are blatantly evil, has short-term payoffs to the user as well as costs. Anger has its cheap thrill; envy and jealousy may stimulate persons to constructive action. Bondage to fear allows a person to avoid discomfort. Drug use may provide escape or thrills and provide companionship (usually superficial and temporary) by allowing the user to be part of a group. Each disorder, each variety of sin, provides partial fulfillment of needs. If they did not they would not be as popular as they are.

We saw Bram choose to stifle his feelings rather than risk rejection. Later, when pressure built up he would explode. In both cases he got some payoffs. He thought these were beneficial to him but they weren't.

What may seem to be a benefit (e.g., physical pleasure in an affair) is not beneficial because it encourages repetition of an inherently destructive system of need fulfillment. False "benefits" don't last; they hide the costs and they give the illusion that the system of need fulfillment (which may become a disorder of self-control) is valid. They are dangerous because they encourage the person to keep the distorted system.

Teaching by a counselor and "opening of the eyes" by the Holy Spirit can lead the disordered person to recognize that the payoffs aren't good enough. They can learn and use systems of fulfillment that are effective.

COSTS OF DEFECTIVE FULFILLMENT SYSTEMS

The costs are far larger than the benefits. Anger, envy, and jealousy drive other people away. Bondage to fear leads to missing out on enjoyable activities. Drug and alcohol abuse take a horrible toll on physical health, financial stability, job performance, and family relationships. Each disorder has costs.

If the activity system is sinful, it alienates the person from God's blessings. It creates barriers to enjoying fellowship with other believers and slows progress toward Christian maturity.

Bram alienated his family, lived in fear on the job, and was dissatisfied with himself. Costs like these are part of every self-control disorder.

Costs are harmful in and of themselves, and they multiply. For example, a jealous person becomes lonely and begins drinking. This leads to difficulty at work, deterioration of other relationships, and symptoms of depression such as insomnia. In response, he or she drinks more, increasing the problems and leading to intense conflict and anger.

There can be a constructive outcome from the costs. When they get severe enough the pain may lead the person to evaluate the activity system and decide that the payoffs are not worth the costs. This is the turning point that is commonly called "hitting bottom." It is a necessary step in correcting every disorder of self-control.

REPETITIONS

If a system works reasonably well, people generally repeat it. The bad choice will be made again and again until better choices are known and seem attractive. Bram had cycled through his system many times. People repeat defective systems even when they believe that "there must be more to life than this." They do so when the payoffs (whether real or illusory) outweigh the costs, or when they do not know an alternative, or in situations where strong peer pressure is exerted to continue the system, or because of a great fear of trying something new, or because they are in physical or emotional addiction (bondage to sin).

In counseling you will be able to offer them the good news of the gospel, and the joyous lifestyle Christians can have. Instruction on how to break habits, with support and accountability for doing so, are valuable at this point.

DISORDER OF SELF-CONTROL

When an ineffective system for fulfillment is repeated even though costs outweigh payoffs the person has a disorder. Now, in addition to being a problem, it creates new problems. For example, job disruption for the alcoholic, burdening debt for the impulsive spender, punishment for the apprehended shoplifter, or alienation for the explosive. The disorder is the result of a long series of decisions made on the basis of erroneous beliefs. The essential element in resolution is that the person recognize the deadliness of the disorder. Such reversal of attitude most often comes at the point the person "hits bottom," but it can come much sooner when a friend (perhaps in the role of counselor, perhaps not) offers God's redemptive love.

We have seen Bram in crisis, with his history of problems, despair about the present, and fear of the future. We have seen where problems such as his originate. Chapter 4 will organize this into a sequence that shows us how to help bring resolution of these disorders.

CHAPTER FOUR

RESOLVING THE PROBLEM

IF YOU TOUR AN AUTOMOBILE ASSEMBLY PLANT you will be impressed with the systematic progression of steps that lead to the finished product. Chapter 3 was somewhat like that, starting with a basic framework and adding, in developmental sequence, the influences that lead to the final state of a disorder of self-control.

Counseling a person with disordered self-control is much different than describing that person's developmental history. Counseling is much more like a body repair shop where wrecked cars are rebuilt than like an assembly plant. Rebuilding wrecked cars is never the same twice and certain things must be undone before others can be done.

This chapter is a "repair of accident damage" chapter. We will use the understanding gained in chapter 3, but the sequence is much different because we must be able to meet the needs as they are brought to us.

When I read books on counseling I marvel at the precision of the examples. The process always seems so orderly, the issues resolved so efficiently. It is never quite that tidy in my counseling room and it may not be for you, either. During the course of counseling we rarely understand things as fully or as clearly as we do later. That's okay. We don't need to understand it all at once, but we *do* need a "game plan." This chapter describes seven stages in the healing of disorders of self-control. They provide a "game plan" that will help you pray, plan, and counsel effectively.

Before we study the seven stages, let's consider two topics that are not compartmentalized within them: evangelism and the relationship between counselor and client. Evangelism (explicitly teaching about salvation and inviting decision) may be appropriate in any of the stages, or in none of them, as the Holy Spirit directs. In contrast to this, the counselor's relational style shows forth the life of Christ in the counselor through every moment of the seven stages.

EVANGELISM DURING COUNSELING

The purpose of Christian counseling is to help the client know and follow God. The seventh stage in our counseling sequence, "Growth Toward Christian Maturity," emphasizes this although the phrase could just as well describe the encompassing goal of Christian counseling.

It is especially joyous when a client makes a commitment of faith during counseling. But your client's salvation is not *fully* your responsibility. It is not for you to try to regiment salvation or organize evangelism by formula. It is your duty to pray for your client's salvation and to follow the Holy Spirit's call to witness, but trying to *impose* salvation onto your client is an effort to usurp the work of the Holy Spirit whose task it is to orchestrate God's overtures to your client. Even Paul, the fervent evangelist, used much of his time teaching about subjects other than salvation.

Be ready to talk with persons about the meaning of God's mercy and grace in your own life. You always can and should do this. You can not, *not* do it! People know your life view and your level of maturity from their experience of you. The question is not *whether* to communicate your faith to the client, but *how.* With this client, today, do you speak explicitly about salvation? Do you encourage a decision? Urge a decision? Or are your words, permeated by your faith, directed toward other matters?

For answers to these questions, listen for counsel from the Holy Spirit. Be ready to speak or not to speak about this matter or that matter, rather than following a formula. Put obedience to God's agenda at the top of your "to do" list.

Be able to present the plan of salvation clearly and easily if the Holy Spirit prompts you. That might be first in your sequence of activities with that client, or eighth, or not part of your experience with that client at all. Or, a systematic presentation of salvation doctrine might be taught in bits and pieces during the counseling process.

Direct the counseling process as seems best to you. Know that God, who loves you and your client immeasurably, will guide you in every part of it.

THE COUNSELOR/CLIENT RELATIONSHIP

People enter counseling wanting to be accepted and understood. If you show that you genuinely care about them and wish to understand the needs of their heart as accurately as you can, they will tell them to you. People talk when it's safe to do so. You can provide this safety by showing acceptance and hope.

The counselee's first reward for being in counseling is *acceptance.* This should be evident to him or her in the first minutes of conversation and usually brings emotional relief. You show acceptance through attentive listening without judgment. As you do this, you learn more about what is going on and the circumstances that have led up to it.

When you understand how things are for this person and how he or she came to be this way, you will be able to guide the counseling toward healing and wholeness. Not before. Prove your love by nonjudgmental acceptance of the persons' worth as individuals despite their behavior, even when (perhaps *especially* when) that behavior is repugnant to you.

What you *don't* do is equally important! Avoid judgment of the person's behavior; they've probably had an abundance of that from friends and family. If you are shocked, try not to show this. Don't be domineering, or arrogant. Take care to not let the conversation stay on trivial topics, and don't give the appearance, through careless posture or low eye contact, that you are disinterested. Experienced counselors find that they need to continue to monitor themselves carefully to avoid these mistakes.

To clarify your thinking and to find gaps of information you need, write a summary of the case. Include your understanding of the person's feelings and his or her view of the origin and prognosis of the disorder. State your own. State your perception of how the disorder affects other people and describe the obstacles to resolution. Review this before your next conversation with the counselee.

The counselee's second reward is *hope*. For the person with a disorder of self-control, hope for change is based in God's healing power, but persons who have spun around and around in their cycles of dyscontrol are usually rather skeptical about that. Hope must become tangible, and it does so in the relationship with the counselor. Acceptance by the counselor brings hope that the disorder can be endured, but this level of hope is not enough. The counselor must produce evidence of ability to guide the individual in resolving the root problems. By the end of the first session the counselor should be able to explain how problems like his or hers begin and how they can be resolved. But hope must not be given carelessly. It is cruel and dishonest to offer a person something that can't happen. When talking about the processes of change, take care to be realistic about the time and effort the counselee will probably invest.

HOW TO HELP: THE ISAIAH 6:10 SEQUENCE

Christian counseling is a combination of friendship and teaching, guided by God's principles and empowered by his love, with the goal of facilitating another person's spiritual, emotional, and relational healing and growth. Counseling is never the same twice because the Holy Spirit does not operate according to human equations. (Aren't you glad that Michelangelo was not limited to a paint-by-number kit!)

Your experience may not be exactly as described in this chapter, but the process of resolving disorders of self-control usually involves seven stages, which are summarized in Table 1.

The first stage is crisis management to protect the disordered person and family members from further harm. When this is needed, it obviously should be first. Chapter 5 describes these processes of "emotional first aid."

Stages 2 through 6 were stated by the Lord as he commissioned Isaiah. Set within a message of solemn judgment upon the Israelites is a prescription for healing which they had rejected:

Make the heart of this people calloused;
   make their ears dull
   and close their eyes.
Otherwise they might *see with their eyes,*
   hear with their ears,
   understand with their hearts,
and turn and be healed.   (Isa. 6:10 italics added)

Chapters 6–18 show how you can help persons see, hear, understand, turn, and be healed.

The seventh stage is growth toward Christian maturity. This is the transition from remediation into the lifelong process of becoming more like our Savior, Jesus Christ. Chapters 19 and 20 instruct about this. For each stage, I will describe responsibilities and activities for the client and the counselor, and show how we can collaborate with God in the healing process. This will be illustrated by continuing the case study of Bram from chapter 2.

Understanding the typical sequence gives you "guideposts" and may help you be patient with the client, locate gaps of information and understanding (so you can get more data from the client and more wisdom from the Lord), and pray warmly and wisely about the counseling.

The Isaiah 6:10 Sequence in Counseling

Stage 1: Manage the Crisis
Client input
　Physically accessible and at least minimally compliant
Counselor processes
　First aid
　Protection

Stage 2: See relationships that model health
Client input
　Is socially accessible
Counselor processes
　Demonstrates reliability and competence
　Fosters support for the client

Stage 3: Hear truth about self and living
Client input
　Describes what is going on
　Considers truth
Counselor processes
　Listens to client
　Exposes client to truth

Stage 4: Understand the disorder
Client input
　Disclosure in depth
Counselor processes
　Identifies costs, payoffs and root problems
　Uses IDEAS diagram

Stage 5: Turn toward health
Client input
　Accepts responsibility for problem
　Accepts responsibility for change
　Learns and uses coping skills
Counselor processes
　Shows client responsibility clearly
　Teaches coping skills
　Teaches new life patterns

Stage 6: Be healed
Client input
　Collaborates fully in resolution of root problems, which may involve confession and
　　repentance, apology, restitution, forgiving
　Changes habits
Counselor processes
　Guides resolution of root problems
　Fosters fulfillment of needs

Stage 7: Grow in Christian maturity
Client input
　Manages behavior
　Manages residual problems
Counselor processes
　Teaching
　Christian discipling

Table 1

47

CHAPTER FIVE

CRISIS MANAGEMENT IN DISORDERS OF SELF-CONTROL

CONSTRUCTIVE CHANGE USUALLY BEGINS at a time of crisis. This can be a "window of opportunity" for friends or counselors to help a person launch the change process.

Sometimes the stress of crisis is so extreme, and the person's resources for dealing with it are so overwhelmed, that the distressed person tries to cause physical or emotional injury to self or others. Management is needed or there will be more distress.[1]

STAGE 1: CRISIS MANAGEMENT

The first objective of crisis management is to prevent a harmful situation from becoming worse. The second objective is to influence the distressed person to find resolution for the root causes of the problem.

The methods used to meet the first objective are highly directive. In the more extreme situations methods may include physical restraint, medication, or forced commitment to a resident treatment program. In less intense situations they may include strong verbal commands, confrontation by loved ones or persons in power (e.g., employer, coach), or simply taking the person away from the place of stress.

All of these methods are aided by a relationship that demonstrates love and respect. Indeed, physical force without visible respect usually incites a strong physical reaction. Empathy and respect can be persuasive even during intense conflict. Miami Police Chief Bernard Garmire says, "It doesn't take a hard-core crime fighter to deal with 80 percent of our calls, but it does take people with compassion, empathy, and ability."[2] Accomplishing the second objective is also aided or hindered by the quality of relationship between the distressed person and the helpers.

Counseling is a sequence of trust, involvement, and growth. The disordered person chooses to trust the helper, allows the helper to be involved, and this results in growth. The sequence—trust, involvement, growth—may be repeated many times as increasing trust allows involvement in more sensitive or more hidden areas of life.

When crisis management is needed, the helper's involvement is quite active and may seem to be the dominant feature of helping; but trust still comes first. The presence of trust marks the difference between a hurting person taking part in the helping process, and his or her being controlled.

A CRISIS MANAGEMENT SYSTEM

Crisis management follows the Isaiah 6:10 sequence, but condenses the chain of events in time. Often there is a high level of emotional intensity. Let us list the most important counselor actions in each stage:

See
    The counselor offers realistic hope, shows love.

Hear
> The counselor listens without judgment, seeking to gather helpful information.

Understand
> The counselor defines the problems, needs, and alternative actions.

Turn
> The counselee (if possible) or counselor chooses the actions that are best for the client.

Be healed
> The actions are implemented.

Dos and Don'ts of Crisis Management

Several attitudes and methods are important in crisis management:[3]

1. Show respect. Affirm the person for everything they have done well. Show empathy in some of your early statements. In some studies, advice-giving has been rated most favorably when it was preceded by empathy.[4]

2. Do not belittle counselees or dispute their perception of how things are. They may be upset over what seems to you a trivial matter. If it is a small concern, they will understand that later in counseling.

3. Look for root causes. Crisis management may bring dramatic relief promptly, but will be short-lived unless the root causes are remedied. If the gas tank on your car is leaking we might get you back on the highway quickly by filling your empty tank, but it will soon be empty again unless you plug the hole. That takes longer. Start thinking right away about how attention can be given to the root causes.

4. Do not be impatient. Counseling on disorders of self-control is often a lengthy process. You and the counselee usually will not understand the chain of events that has led to the crisis until several sessions have passed or perhaps only after many sessions. Crisis management makes it possible for counselees to invest time and energy, finding and resolving the root problems.

Crisis management may need doing before you have time to build a relationship, but it is a chance to begin building one—

to prove that you can understand, be trusted, and that your ideas are sensible and will work. This earns you the opportunity to go on.

5. Focus on actions that can be taken, not on past events.

6. Do not do for persons what they can do for themselves. Help them capitalize on their own strengths to help themselves. Typically, the more you do the less they do, and the less they do the less likely it is that changes will last. Your aim is to help persons change, not to change the persons. Necessary dependency during crisis is acceptable, but your goal is to help them become properly independent.

7. Respond to anger properly. When people are angry they tend to be more suspicious and defensive, so you will want to be careful how you respond. Your most important verbal message is assurance that, "It's okay for you to feel angry. I want to hear what you have to say and I will help you if I can." In most cases this acceptance does more than any other one thing you can do because it shows your respect and caring, which builds hope. Keep your words simple, short, clear, and honest.

Your nonverbal style will be a bit different than usual. When you have the other person's attention, talk softly, slowly, and distinctly. Avoid sudden or dramatic body movements and do not crowd his space.

8. Be careful about using physical touch. It is usually welcomed during sorrow, risky during anger.

9. Don't wade into an explosive situation. Twenty-five percent of police deaths and 40 percent of the injuries come during responses to domestic crises. However, physical violence, even among cases in which police are called, is the exception rather than the rule.[5] We should not be intimidated, but neither should we depart from common-sense cautiousness.

10. Refer to community resources willingly.

11. Don't scold yourself if you can't help as much as you might like. If you can't do it all, this is not your responsibility (1 Cor. 3:5–9).

Illustration from Bram

Pastor Hart knew that Bram carried a lot of internal tension. Glenda had only hinted about it and Bram would not talk about it—but it showed. At 9:30 one Friday evening Glenda called, crying, and said, "Bram's hysterical. He's having a tantrum and we don't know what he's going to do next. It's the worst it's ever been." Bram's voice in the background, loud and peppered with profanity, ordered Glenda to get off the phone. "Please come over," she whispered.

"Do both of you want me to come?" the pastor asked.

"I don't think so."

"I will come, but I would prefer if Bram were in favor of it, too. Would you ask him if it would be all right for me to come?"

"I don't want to do that."

"Please do."

Pastor Hart heard Bram muttering in the background but couldn't distinguish what he was saying. Then Glenda returned to the phone.

"It's all right with him. Please hurry."

As Pastor Hart drove, his head swirled with conflicting thoughts and impulses: *They need specialized help that I'm not trained to give. How can I be serious about praying for them, as I have, if I'm not responsive when they need me? Bram really doesn't want me there. This could drive him away from the church forever. Glenda wants me there, which might anger Bram. He might hurt me. The Lord is in control. No, in that house right now, Bram is in control. No, the Lord is in control and I can trust him to guide me.*

New thoughts, pro and con, were still emerging when he rang the Wilnocks' doorbell. Glenda invited him in. "Bram's in the basement. I don't know what he's doing; I only know what mood he's in. When he gets mad, that's where he goes."

They heard boxes and boards being moved and stacked, punctuated by the sound of a glass jar shattering on the concrete floor in a shower of sharp-edged obscenities. Glenda went downstairs and the pastor heard two muffled voices in urgent debate. The two came upstairs.

Bram, head down and tight lipped, sat at the opposite end of the sofa from Pastor Hart's tentative perch and said, "I'm sorry she asked you to come over. Not that I mind, but it just wasn't necessary. She gets over-excited some times, that's all there is to it."

"That's *not* all there is to it," Glenda sobbed. "I admit, I've been yelling, but I'm scared and I'm scared of you. It wouldn't matter, except I love you."

"Love me!" Bram yelled. "You said you wanted to leave! You call that love?"

"I didn't say I *wanted* to."

Bram jumped to his feet. "If you want to leave, you leave! You hear *that* everybody?"

Glenda curled forward in her chair, face in her hands, and silently poured bitter tears into her hands. Bram stood motionless, staring at her. Pastor Hart sat rigidly. It was as though the flames of conflict had fired everyone into ceramic statues.

Pastor Hart spoke with quiet calm, warmth and authority in his voice. "Bram and Glenda, I thank you both for letting me be with you now. You both must be feeling a great amount of pain right now. That can change. It's a hard time, but it can lead to better times. I want to ask permission to stay long enough for us to talk about how we might use this time to the benefit of both of you. Okay?"

Glenda said, "Okay."

Bram turned slowly to look down at Pastor Hart, who said, "Bram, what I'd like would be to listen to whatever you want to tell me for a little bit and then see if we can't figure out how things can improve. I am sure they can. But I don't want to be here unless it's okay with you. Is it?"

"Yeah, that's okay."

"You could just sit over there again, and I'll be here, and we can just talk straight out about the things that are important to you."

Bram sat down, restlessly rubbing his hands. "I really hate to put you out, you as busy as you are."

"If I can be helpful to you, I *want* to be. You know why I want to?"

Bram said, "No."

"Because I get a lot of satisfaction out of seeing people's lives get better."

"We're not doing so bad. I get edgy, yeah, and even kind of noisy and ugly now and then, like this. I admit that, but. . . ." He paused, pushing his hands into the cracks between the sofa cushions. He leaned toward Glenda, glaring angrily and snarled, "But I *hate* it when the people around here don't help out like they ought to. You think that. . . ."

Pastor Hart tapped Bram's arm, and said, "I'd *like* to hear about how things are and how you'd like for things to be. Could you and I just sit here by ourselves and talk? I want to see if I can understand, because I think that if we both understand it we can find some ways to make things better for everyone."

"I don't mind if she leaves the room. She wants to leave my *life*, I think."

Glenda walked away, slowly and quietly.

"Bram, please tell me what *you* want."

"Reverend, all I want is for them to appreciate me a little bit. For them to show it by helping out a little. Just a simple thank you and a helping hand now and then would be nice; but no, they're too busy for that."

"You work hard; I know you do. You want some credit for that."

"Is that too much to ask?"

"I don't think so. I like that, too."

"See? That's what I told her. But, boy oh boy, she just brushed that off and that's when I blew up."

"You blew up."

"Uh, yeah."

"Which, I suppose, shows how painful getting brushed off can be."

"Yeah."

"To you, that is. We're not talking about everybody. We're talking about you. So when she brushed off what you said, that was *extremely* painful. For *you.*"

"Oh, yeah. It set me off pretty good." He laughed, a nervous, self-conscious laugh that seemed layered with shame.

"What's that like, for you?"

"I don't like it."

"Is that something you want to be different in the future?"

"Yeah."

"It can be."

"Well, tell her how to do it."

"Bram, I'm pretty sure there are some things that Glenda ought to do differently. I would like to talk with her about those things. Same for you, of course—some things you could do a little differently." He smiled and said, "It doesn't surprise you that I think that, does it?"

Bram smiled a bit and said, "Heck no. What are preachers for?"

"Sometime when it's convenient for you," Hart continued, "maybe next Monday or Tuesday, let's talk about *that* stuff. Can we?"

"If it don't take too long."

"Let's say half an hour. Want to meet here, stop by the church on the way home, or what?"

"I'll come by the church at 5:30, if it's okay."

"Super! Let's talk a minute with Glenda and then I'll get going." When Glenda joined them, Pastor Hart said that it seemed to him that both of them wanted good things *from* the other, and wanted good things *for* the other. "That being the case, the two of you can learn what you need to learn about the painful spots in your lives, and the marriage, and with God's help you can fix those spots." He mentioned the appointment with Bram. "We're just going to get better acquainted, and I'm really looking forward to that."

"Sounds good," Glenda said.

Pastor Hart nodded agreement. "Are *you* committed to doing your part, just as Bram is committed to doing *his* part?"

"Yes."

"Great! Then would you come in next week, by yourself, too?" They set an appointment.

"That's all well and good for next week," Pastor Hart, concluded, "but what is most important for right now?"

Bram spoke at once. "I just want to know that somehow, someday, things are going to be better!"

"Fair enough. Glenda, what's important for you right now?"

"The same thing. To know that we're going to get through it and come out with a marriage we both enjoy."

"Wow! I like the sound of that! Both of you are headed in

exactly the right direction. The Lord has helped us tonight and will in the future. We have a plan which begins next week. Before I go, I think we should tie up the loose ends from this evening. Can we do that?"

Pastor Hart led them into reconciling the conflict of the evening, affirming them for their cooperation and commitment in doing so, and closed in prayer. They all went to bed tired, but with optimism. Systematic counseling with Bram began the next week, although Bram didn't think of it as counseling until many months after it was over.

This scenario illustrates, in very condensed form, **several** crisis-management methods and principles: Pastor **Hart** showed respect, love, and competence. He took charge without belittling Bram or Glenda. He used their statements of commitment to demonstrate that they have hope and to dilute the immediate tension. They agreed on a plan that would lead to healing the root problems.

Many months after the crisis visit, Bram said, "Pastor, I'm curious about something. That time when I was so worked up and Glenda called you, you had her ask me if you could come over. I said okay, but what would you have done if I had said no?"

Pastor: I would have told Glenda to tell you that I wanted to talk to you on the phone and that if you didn't talk on the phone I would come over.

Bram: Suppose I hadn't talked on the phone?

Pastor: I would have asked Glenda if she was afraid someone would be physically hurt. If she said yes, then I would have called the police, driven to your house first and waited for them, and then I would have asked them to let me go in ahead of them.

If she had said no, she wasn't afraid, I would have gone back to bed and looked you up at the shop the next day.

Bram: If you had, I'd have been nice like usual, but suppose I would have been ugly with you?

Pastor: All I could do would be to offer you my friendship. That's all God can do with us—offer. We can't do more, either. Sometimes, we do all we can and it doesn't seem to be helpful. That's painful. I really don't like that. Sometimes all I can do is be responsive to the opportunity and leave it at that. I'm glad you have taken God and me up on our offers of friendship!

Bram: Yeah!

SUMMARY

Crisis management is not enough. Management, without resolving the root problem, is like moving from one room to another in a burning hotel. Temporary relief is fine, but not good enough.

It is strategic, however, and may be our complete response in a particular case. David asked God to let him build the temple; but Solomon built it (Acts 7:46,47). We do not do all of the worthy things that we might like to do, and that is all right. If you intervene with crisis management in persons' lives and help them enter counseling, you have been helpful. Celebrate this opportunity to have been of service!

CHAPTER SIX

COUNSELING AND THE PROBLEM: SEE, HEAR

CHAPTER 5 DESCRIBED WAYS to "stop the flow of blood" and care for the wounded in times of emotional crisis. We do not always enter the life of a hurting person at a time of crisis. If we are attentive and caring with people who come into our lives, the ordinary development of friendship will reveal that some of them have disorders of self-control or other distress in their lives and we will have the opportunity to help.

This is illustrated by a recent experience. I went into a barber shop with four barbers: three men and a woman. The woman's chair was open so I sat down and closed my eyes to relax while she worked. We had this conversation:

Betty: Are you on your way to work?

Rich: No. I work at home.

Betty: What do you do?

Rich: At the present, I am writing full time.

Betty: Do you write novels?

Rich: No. I'm a psychologist, so I write nonfiction in that field.

Betty: I've been a single parent for thirteen years and that's really been difficult!

Wham! She had gone from small talk to a cry for help the fourth time she spoke, so I showed my interest. She said that her father was an alcoholic and that she had married a man just like him; she expressed fear that his disorder had hurt their children (wounds and deficits) and that now, as young adults, they would not make good decisions.

When I told her that our church (of one hundred twenty-five members) sponsors a group for adult children of alcoholics, she was interested. I told her how to get in touch with Whitey, the coordinator.

Last week I had a strong sense that I should go back to the barber shop and make sure Betty had talked with Whitey. On the way I prayed that I would be able to talk with her. Again, her chair was open. She had called the wrong place and hadn't found Whitey, but said it would be all right for him to call her at the shop. He did. Since she cannot attend the meetings, Whitey is "connecting" her with a Christian woman in the group who can listen, understand, encourage, support, advise, and witness. We don't know what will happen, but Betty will hear how God can heal her life.

This illustrates three things: (1) Chances for ministry may come when we least expect them; (2) our part in the helping process is sometimes a brief but necessary link, and (3) hurting persons need to see the gospel in human flesh. If we are Christian they should see the gospel in us; if we are in community we may be able to connect the hurting person with others in whom they can see Christ, hear of his healing power, and understand how they can have personal healing and growth. "Seeing" is where change usually begins.

STAGE 2: SEE RELATIONSHIPS THAT MODEL HEALTH

When persons with disorders of self-control see people living effectively it may generate hope and conviction, and motivate them toward change. Let us look at the counselor and client contributions in this stage.

Counselor Process

1. *Demonstrates reliability and competence.* When counseling on problems of self-control it is essential that the counselor be unquestionably trustworthy. It is no less important in other stages, with clients who have other problems; nor is it less imperative when we are not in a counseling role than when we are. Persons with disorders of self-control may reject truth and discipline with the slightest excuse. Don't give them one.

2. *Fosters support for the client.* Counselors who have strong connections with a body of Christians can, with the counselee's cooperation, surround him or her with people who live effectively and offer wholesome alternatives to the disordered behavior. All of these can support the counselee without supporting the disorder.

Ask yourself: How can the client become more involved with church life?[1] Who can become a friend and life-style model? What support might be provided to family members?

Counselee Input: Is Socially Accessible

We help the disordered person become involved with healthy people in constructive social activities. Since harmony with others is a normal need, this isn't calling for much investment from the person.

Illustration from Bram

Glenda had used good judgment with Bram, encouraging him toward social activity in the church but not making it a burden. Bram saw some examples of Christian maturity and noticed some hypocrisy, too. He had once said, "they don't all live up to what they believe, but they believe in a pretty high standard and most of them come up to it fairly close."

The pastor had been able to "connect" with Bram personally

and this paid off when Bram was ready to change. Give Glenda and the pastor high marks for helping Bram spend time with people who live effectively.

STAGE 3: HEAR TRUTH ABOUT SELF AND LIVING

It is not enough to be exposed to truth; one must use it. A milestone in the resolution of a self-control disorder is the transition from just blankly staring at truth to considering how to act upon it. This may not seem like much of a distinction, but it is a vital one. Counselee input and counselor processes allow this to happen.

Counselee Input: Describes What Is Going On

This afternoon I met a young man for the first time. He said, "I don't think I'm going to be able to talk about what went on a year ago. It's so silly and I'm really embarrassed about it, and, anyway, I don't think it matters anymore. Even if I tried to talk about it, it would take at least two hours."

"Could you give me a five-minute sample of it?" I asked. "It would be helpful to hear at least a few highlights so we can then put it aside if it's not important."

He did. And it was important. He knew that, and he had wanted to talk about it from the outset. People always want to talk about what is important to them. When they are reluctant it is nearly always because they are not yet sure they can trust us. Prove that they can, and they will talk.

Counselor Process

1. Listens to client. The quality of our listening, more than any other thing, determines the individual's level of comfort in talking with us.[2] Early in counseling, people often complain about their discomforts and unmet needs, and blame others for these problems. As we offer understanding and compassion, we form hunches about the counselee's beliefs, root conditions, and why he or she believes the disordered actions can be beneficial.

Early in most sessions, and especially while getting to know a person, a high percentage of my statements will paraphrase what the client has said (in the manner of Rogerian nondirective responses). I find that this helps me keep attention on the clients, show acceptance, and it makes it easy for them to talk.

2. Exposes client to truth. I am not willing to be nondirective in the presence of untruth! It is important to me to affirm God's truth, to call clients to question the validity of their own statements, and to show cause-and-effect relationships with vivid accuracy. This is done as gently and lovingly as possible so it will have the greatest chance to "stick."[3]

Counselee Input: Considers Truth

As counselees observe us (or other people who are living effectively) they think about how their own lives might improve. This may be the beginning of change. They may engage in structured counseling which can be a great step forward even when they do not admit the need to change or commit to the processes of change.

Illustration from Bram

This is from Bram's first session with the pastor.

1. Bram: You know how Glenda gets a little upset about how I act sometimes. Personally, I think she overreacts. But I said I'd come and talk, even if I don't think it's important enough to bother you with.

2. Pastor: I'm *glad* we can talk. If it's important to either one of you, it's good for us to talk about it. There is nothing I'd rather do in the next forty-five minutes than have this time with you.

3. Bram: I don't want her to make a mountain out of a molehill.

4. Pastor: I appreciate that. And yet there's something that looks like a mountain to her even if it doesn't to you.

5. Bram: Yeah, that's about the way it is.

6. Pastor: I'd *really* like for us to talk about it, because I think we can find some answers that would be good for you and Glenda.

7. Bram: Okay, let's do it. Where do you want me to start?

8. Pastor: You can start wherever you'd like, perhaps by just describing what has been happening in your own life.

The pastor nurtures the spark of interest that Bram shows (2, 4), affirms him (2, 6), and expresses confidence that it can be worthwhile to talk (6).

9. Bram: I know I get a little overexcited sometimes. They just don't know how much pressure I'm under.
10. Pastor: You're feeling a *lot* of pressure.
11. Bram: Oh, boy! Yeah! At work. We just get busier and busier, and more and more parts change all the time.
12. Pastor: It must seem overwhelming sometimes.
13. Bram: Most of the time. *(Pause)* Most of the time. But that's no excuse for me acting the way I do at home.
14. Pastor: That sounds like you're feeling pretty bad about it yourself.

Comments: The pastor's responses 10, 12, and 14 paraphrase Bram's statements, proving that the pastor has listened accurately. This encourages Bram to say more, as seen in 11, 13, and 15.

15. Bram: They don't like it when I get upset. Well, I don't either. I don't like it, but I think I have my reasons. They don't put out the kind of cooperation that they should, to help me when I come home tired. But I don't know what to do about it.
16. Pastor: Let me make sure I understand what you've said so far. You said you're under pressure, and sometimes you blow up at home. They don't like it, and you don't either.
17. Bram: Right.
18. Pastor: You're uptight and unhappy, but you don't know how to change it.
19. Bram: Right.
20. Pastor: That's how things are *now*. How do you want things to be *different?*
21. Bram: I want *them* to do *their* share of the load. To take care of *their* things, so they don't set me off.
22. Pastor: For example.

23. Bram: You know how it was the time you came over to the house. They don't do their share, like Ginny not taking care of that dang litter box!

24. Pastor: Yes.

25. Bram: They should pay more attention to what happens to *me!*

26. Pastor: To understand your pressure?

27. Bram: Sure!

28. Pastor: And?

29. Bram: Well, that's all I ask. Just for them to take care of their responsibilities and to give me a little respect. That should pretty well fix everything up okay.

30. Pastor: Those are good things that you want from them.

31. Bram: Reasonable enough, I think.

32. Pastor: Yes, it's fair enough for you to want them to respect you and understand what you go through, and to cooperate.

33. Bram: Yeah!

34. Pastor: And, in turn, there would be some things you would want to be sure you were offering them. What are those?

35. Bram: I've been a pretty good provider. I work hard.

36. Pastor: I've been impressed—maybe I should say amazed—at what you do. When I've seen you at the shop, it has just about blown me away to see the complexity of your work. When you talk about the pressure there I think I understand that because I've seen how much you have to keep track of there and I saw one of the mechanics get pretty abusive to you when you didn't have the part he wanted.

37. Bram: That's how it is, all right, and that's not all there is to it.

38. Pastor: You've given great efforts for your family in your work, and I really respect you for that! Let's shift over to a more personal part of life and check that out. How would you rate yourself in regard to listening to Glenda and the kids, so that you can understand and appreciate them?

39. Bram: Frankly, I'm not very good at that.
40. Pastor: What do you want to do about that?

Comments: The pastor listens well and affirms Bram when appropriate, but wants Bram to go beyond venting his frustration. Statement 38 shifts attention to Bram, and in 39 he takes responsibility. This is quite different than at 15 when Bram was blaming them. Capitalizing on this, the pastor seeks to agree on a plan.

41. Bram: I'm always willing to do my part.
42. Pastor: In this situation, what would your part be?
43. Bram: I could listen to them better than I do. Probably I could lay off of some of my criticizing them. I criticize Todd and Ginny quite a bit, I think. Glenda, too. I could do less of that.
44. Pastor: That's terrific! I think they would like that a lot. How would you go about that?
45. Bram: They are usually home when I get back from work, so I could just ask them how things are going. And then keep my mouth shut instead of giving an opinion on everything.
46. Pastor: Yes! Okay then, you have a plan to change one part of the whole thing. You do that, and that's a great beginning! We both know that's not all there is to it, but this would be a great start because you'd know that you are doing what you can to support them. There are a lot of other things we will want to talk about, and ways to make improvement, one by one, just like you are going to make this improvement.

Comment: The pastor identified a portion of the problem and described it to Bram, who not only heard but committed himself to change. This is a lot of progress on a small part of the total problem. It is not enough, because it deals only with relational style and not the root problems. But, if Bram offers more kindness within the family there may be more tranquility during the time Bram is working toward a healing of the root problems.

CHAPTER SEVEN

COUNSELING AND THE PROBLEM: UNDERSTAND

THE CRISIS IS UNDER CONTROL. The counselor has a relationship of trust with the counselee and has fostered supportive relationships. The counselee is describing the present circumstances and considering truth that applies to it. Now they can find the origins of and solutions for the disorder.

STAGE 4: UNDERSTAND THE DISORDER

The counselor shifts now from talking about God's healing for *people*, to God's healing for the *counselee*. This requires access to the most sensitive information about the person's life, which is rarely divulged except in a relationship of deep trust. When counselors do not have solutions to problems it is often because they do not understand the situation, which is due to a failure to create conditions in which the person has felt free to talk.

Counselee Input: Disclosure in Depth

The counselee needs to tell it all—to follow the lead of the Holy Spirit and the counselor into the attitudes, past events, idolatrous desires, or whatever else may be root problems. The counselor may need to push the counselee into topics or personal history he or she would rather avoid.

If the relationship provides trust and respect the counselee will collaborate, but it requires courage and determination. The counselor will give encouragement, and the counselee will take risks to the extent the counselor has shown integrity and competence. Finding the root problems may require investigating material he or she has repressed. Repression is the mental process of removing painful ideas, memories, or impulses from conscious awareness. It is done without deliberation, and serves to protect the person from discomfort.

Anything that has been so hurtful to us that we have hidden it from ourselves *may* have the power to hurt us again when it is brought back in the open. Therefore, we are usually willing to uncover repressed painful emotions and memories only in the company of a trusted friend and with the help of the Holy Spirit.[1]

Counselor Process

1. Identify the costs. Costs are those consequences that drain emotional energy and are barriers to health and growth. The counselor helps identify the costs and teaches about them without condemning the individual. We want to teach people that the way to change the costs is to eliminate the disorder. We will not reduce the costs by rescuing them from the natural consequences of their behavior. For example, if Bram were arrested for disorderly conduct, we would visit him in jail but probably not post bail.

As you seek to understand people, they will begin listening to you and seeing their lives from your perspective. Eventually they will understand how you view the costs of their disorder of self-control. They may not agree with your opinion, but that is their choice, and you can continue to show your acceptance of *counselees* even when you do not accept or condone their *beliefs* or *behavior.*

People usually tend to minimize the costs. Becoming more realistic about the costs is a sign of growing commitment to change.

2. Identify the payoffs. Payoffs keep a disorder going by giving the illusion that it is better than the alternatives. The counselor helps identify payoffs, exposes them for the fraud they are, and helps the other person discard them. The IDEAS diagram, described in chapter 8, can be helpful in showing that the actual value of the payoffs is much less than the client thought.

We may as well concede that sin has temporary, partially satisfying, payoffs. It is likely to surprise one to hear this from a Christian counselor, but to imply that a disorder of self-control is completely without reward suggests to clients that you think they are totally stupid. Trust and rapport are not built that way!

Clients or counselees are likely to exaggerate the value of the payoffs. You may challenge them to test whether they believe the payoffs are as great as they say they are—but take care not to be argumentative. As a person's estimates of the values become more realistic, he or she shows signs of a growing commitment to change.

3. Identify the root problems. What is accomplished during the first three stages is not enough. It brings relief, and that is fine, of course. An alcoholic returned to drinking after four years of sobriety. After another three years of drinking and countless problems, he quit again. While there was shame and regret over what he described as "my wasted years," there was also gratitude for the interval of sobriety. "At least I had those four good years," he said.

But enduring change is the goal. This happens only with resolution of the root problems. The counselor is responsible to lead the way to the root problems. While a nondirective style is often best during early stages of counseling, a directive approach is better here.

I have described six root problems that can generate disorders of self-control. Only one of these may be operating in a particular case, but often there are two or three and sometimes all six. You help the client identify them by inquiry, aided by the Holy Spirit.

A valuable process is for the individual to pray, "Lord, teach me the things I need to learn about this part of my life." Everyone I have known who has prayed this, with a willingness to learn, has received from God necessary instruction that has led to healing in his or her life, and usually quickly.

The counselor has been nondirective much of the time, and this has brought a lot of material. The counselor sorts this out and develops some hunches about the root problems, shifting to a more directive, systematic probing to discover the roots of the disorder. Here are some suggestions to help you investigate each of the root conditions:

a. *Sinful nature.* Let's not be reluctant to inquire about spiritual matters and offer distinctively Christian responses.[2] In my experience, people have not been uneasy about responding to questions concerning their religious beliefs. In fact, many times I have talked with persons whose friends described as being violently opposed to talking about Christianity, only to find they welcome a discussion of faith. They may not agree, but they will talk and listen.

As with inquiry on any topic, we *start* general and *become* more specific. Some questions that may fit in are: "Was religion part of family life when you were growing up?" "Is religion part of your life now?" "Where are you at with Christianity?" "What does going to church mean to you?" "What does being a Christian mean to you?" "How does being a born-again Christian make a difference in this situation?"

b. *Physiological disadvantages.* Some are obvious (e.g., a paralysis) while other conditions (e.g., learning disorders, effects from a disease, or predisposition to depression) are not visible. Since people come to us expecting to talk about what is important to them, they will not mind inquiries such as: "Please describe your physical condition." "Are there any limitations on what you can do?" "Has there ever been anything physical that has held you back?" "How many years did you go to school?" "What grades did you get?" "Have you had any emotional problems during your life?" "Have any members of your family had psychiatric care?"

Through the course of conversation we make observations of such things as intelligence, ability to communicate, and energy level. We ask questions that help us learn whether there are disadvantages that make the client's life more difficult or less satisfying at the present time.

c. and d. *Deficits and wounds.* We wish to learn about the conditions of childhood.[3] As a child, was the person caressed lovingly and played with, or abused and ignored; told he or she was capable and important, or called helpless and worthless? Was life steady and consistent, or confusing and unpredictable? Did they benefit from good nutrition and medical care or physically fend for themselves?

Questions such as these may be useful: "What did you want as a child that you didn't have?" "What was your father (mother) like?" "As you think back to childhood, what are some of the most powerful memories you have?" "How did your parents respond when you did something wrong?" "How much time did you spend with your mother (father)?" "Who were your best friends during high school (grade school)?"

e. *Discrepancies.* As we listen to counselees we think about the congruence between different parts of their lives. For example, are their attitudes and behavior harmonious with God's design? Will their behavior help them meet their goals? Do they practice what they preach? Are they realistic in expectations?

Are their life views realistic? Do they practice restraint and patience, or pursue immediate gratification? Do they have basic social competencies? Are they honest or conniving? Industrious or lazy? What is the level of their ambition? Do they seek full measure of life's joy, or are they content to settle for the dregs at the bottom of life's cup? These are judgments of evaluation (in contrast to judgments of condemnation) and are legitimate when we are helping a person change.

f. *Consequences of sins.* How is the person different as a result of sins? The consequences may be physical: brain or liver damage resulting from drug or alcohol abuse, incapacitation from drunken driving, or lingering venereal disease. The consequences may be relational: difficulty in trusting others (common among recovering alcoholics), mistrust in a marriage wounded by adultery, or continuing shame about one's past behavior. The consequences are certain to include a sense of distance from God, and perhaps anger toward him. Probe for consequences with gentle specific questions. List them, reminding the client that God has patterns for each that lead toward relief and growth.

Illustration from Bram

This begins at the tenth minute of Bram's second session with his pastor.

47. Pastor: It's important that we identify root causes of the problems we've been talking about. To do that, I'd like to ask you some questions. These will cover a lot of ground, and you can tell me as much or as little as you want to about each. Before we do that, let's pray, asking God to lead us to the things that are important.

They prayed, and the pastor began a process of inquiry. Along the way, the following conversation took place.

48. Pastor: Maybe I'm wrong about this, but it seems to me that talking about your early childhood is difficult.
49. Bram: I was brought up that I shouldn't criticize my parents. They did the best they could.
50. Pastor: Good point. So, we won't criticize them. But it is important and legitimate to *describe* what things were like for *you* during that important part of your life. *Describing* those things will help you understand why you approach life the way you do, and *that* will help you *improve* your life, which is something *they* would want you to do, isn't it?
51. Bram: Oh, yeah. They always wanted what is best for me.
52. Pastor: I believe that *one* of the things that will be good for you now is to understand them better—to

understand the ups and downs from that time in life, so the Lord can help you have healing for the parts that weren't so good.

53. Bram: Okay. That makes sense to me. Well, then, one of the things that I remember is. . . .

Bram needs to look objectively at his parents' weaknesses. The pastor helped overcome feelings of disloyalty about this.

CHAPTER EIGHT

THE IDEAS DIAGRAM: AN AID TO UNDERSTANDING

PEOPLE NEED TO UNDERSTAND THEIR DISORDERS: their costs, payoffs, and actual benefits. They need to recognize how and where they can change the destructive systems they use and compare their present beliefs and actions with alternatives. The counselor needs to sort out a mass of information, trace the development of the disorder, and plan strategies of change.

The method described in this chapter can help you do all of those things. I call this the "IDEAS Diagram" because it shows the connections among Intellection (beliefs, memories, and mental processes), Decision, Emotions, Actions, and Situation. It is a powerful and versatile teaching process that deserves detailed attention.

73

Those familiar with models of cognitive-behavioral counseling will note similarity between this model and others; however, there are several substantial differences. For example, it differs from Rational-Emotive Therapy[1] by being theistic, accepting the existence of absolutes (thereby validating certain shoulds and musts), regarding guilt not as a feeling but as a condition of estrangement from God (that subsequently leads to feelings), and by a greater emphasis on the counselee's capacity to act upon the situation in addition to adapting to it. In these ways it is similar to models of Christian counseling offered by Crabb,[2] Kirwan,[3] Backus,[4] and Worthington.[5]

START WHERE THE PERSON WANTS TO START

People want to feel good. When they seek counseling it usually is because they don't like how they feel and they believe counseling can help them feel better.

The **IDEAS** diagram begins at that point of high motivation. The desire to feel better is an objective the counselor can endorse. He or she can teach first about feelings and show the counselee how beliefs, actions, and conditions have led to painful feelings, then show how more constructive beliefs and actions can lead to better feelings in spite of conditions that are painful.

COMPONENTS OF AN IDEAS DIAGRAM

The diagram links five elements: intellection, decision, emotion, action, and situation. These elements are building blocks you can use to teach people why they feel as they do and why they do what they do. The diagram helps clients understand their past and present, guides them in changing the present and future, and will help the counselor organize the counseling process. We will consider the five words that form the acronym, **IDEAS**.

Intellection encompasses all our mental processes and stored information. It includes our beliefs about: how things *are* (information), how things *should be* (values), how things *could be* (hope), and how things *were* (memories). We are conscious (it is readily accessible) of some of this material, and unconscious (it is pushed aside because it leads to discomfort) of some of it.

Paul stated his belief about the importance of intellectual processes vividly.

> Those who live according to the sinful nature have their minds set on what that nature desires; but those who live in accordance with the Spirit have their minds set on what the Spirit desires. The mind of sinful man is death, but the mind controlled by the Spirit is life and peace, because the sinful mind is hostile to God. It does not submit to God's law, nor can it do so. (Rom. 8:5–7)

According to Paul, who "sets" your mind? You do, and where you set your mind is of life-or-death importance.

Paul also explains that moving from a death consequence to a life consequence begins in the mind. He wrote,

> Do not conform any longer to the pattern of this world, but be transformed by the renewing of your mind. (Rom. 12:2)

Healthy, mature living begins with right thinking. The IDEAS diagram helps you show your clients the consequences of a mind controlled by sin, and how transformation begins by bringing the mind under the direction of the Spirit.

Decision is an internal commitment to a course of action, whether that course of action is taken or not. It is the will stirring a pitcherful of beliefs and emotions and then tipping it in a particular direction, ready to pour a dribble here, or a gush there. Decision is the signal to the hand that is ready to pour; the pouring is action.

Decisions prove our priorities. When we put decisions into action the world knows, imperfectly and incompletely, what God has known perfectly and completely—the intentions of our heart. (See Ps. 44:21 and 1 Thess. 2:4.)

Decision is (1) internal permission; when we make a decision, we are released to act. We may not act, but we could allow ourselves to. It is also (2) a moment. There is a point at which we would say yes, another at which we would say no, and but a split second between. However, this moment is (3) influenced by the lifetime that has preceded it. It is the culmination of our series of choices for or against God's truth. Thus, to understand a person's decision, we must learn a lot about that person, which we do by listening and through the Holy Spirit's counsel to us.

Decision is (4) under our control. It is volitional, influenced by outside forces but never controlled by them. The effects of decisions (5) are cumulative. Repeated bad decisions load the seesaw to the point that we may never get it tipped back the other way. Decision is often so influenced by the unconscious (6) that we may not be aware of the why of a choice, though aware of the choice.

We will first teach people that they are the ones making their decisions. Then we may help them understand the beliefs and emotions that influence their decisions. Sometimes it is necessary to understand the influences that have been repressed, but sometimes that is not necessary or would be impractical.

Emotions are, in everyday terms, how we feel. Persons often believe that their feelings are the result of things that are happening or are not happening to them. Sometimes that is the case. They often believe that they do not have any control over how they feel, but that is not correct. We have considerable influence over our emotions, and to a great extent can change them by changing how we think and how we act. One of the outcomes of successful counseling on disorders of self-control is that the individual has a more satisfying emotional life.

Actions are what we do. Our actions are controlled by our intellection. Before we act, we put our perceptions of the situation, beliefs, emotions, and memories into the "hopper" of our intellection for processing. We consider the options and outcomes; we estimate the risks and rewards. We think about how we would feel about this result compared with that result. Then, and only then, do we decide and act.

In "real life," things happen so fast we usually aren't aware of the sequence, but we always process our thoughts and emotions and make a decision before we act. We *are* in control of our behavior. Sometimes we would rather pretend that we can't be in control; we would deny our responsibility with "the devil made me do it," or, "I couldn't help it." That's nonsense.

God has created us with the capacity for self-control and that is good news! Not only has he given us the capacity for self-control—he helps us learn to use it and he supplements our efforts. Thank you, Lord! Actions may seem to be the problem. They *are* the problem for friends and family members of those who have disorders of self-control, but for the persons themselves, actions are the *symptoms* and *expressions* of the problem, not the problem.

Don't expect that you can change persons' lifestyles by helping them change actions. They believe that the actions of their self-control disorder are beneficial (and to a limited extent they are). They will not change until they believe that a different pattern will be more beneficial. Would you? You may be eager for them to change their actions, and rightly so, because the actions are harmful. But, you may as well put the brakes on that eagerness and concentrate on finding and resolving the root problem.

Situation refers to the things that happen to us. Usually this is closely related to our actions, sometimes not. We may receive an unexpected gift or be attacked at random by a crazed killer, but most of the things that happen to us are influenced by our actions (which are the product of our decisions which are based on intellection which is influenced by emotion). That leaves us in charge, doesn't it? For the most part, yes. Want to improve your situation? Improve your intellection.

At the same time, we each have circumstances in our lives that are beyond our control. These affect us, but the emotional consequences are not beyond our control. Paul attested to the benefits of good thinking and decisions by saying, ". . . I have learned to be content whatever the circumstances" (Phil. 4:11).

USING THE IDEAS DIAGRAM

The IDEAS diagram shows the relationships among the five components. It works best with people who are disciplined enough to work through some of their life "material" in a systematic way. It is helpful in working with those whose motivation is low if they are willing to hear some facts and new ideas. It is not likely to be effective with persons who are in a highly emotional state, mentally confused, or resistant to letting you show them some things about themselves.

Before using IDEAS, build rapport and trust with the counselee. Gather information about the person's situation and emotional and behavioral responses to the situation. Organize some of that in your mind or notes in the IDEAS pattern. You may use the IDEAS diagram in any session, but usually not until the second or third.

Since most people come into counseling because they don't like how they feel and are motivated by the prospect of feeling better, that is where I usually start. Starting where they are (feeling lousy) shows my acceptance of them. I also want to talk as soon as possible about the direction of change (Christian maturity), because that offers hope. My role as counselor, I explain, is to help them know how to get from here to there and to be with them on the journey. Here is the typical sequence in using the diagram:

1. *Define the components of IDEAS.* We will sit so I can write on a pad and both of us can see it easily. Usually I make a carbon copy so the client can have the original and I have one for the file, aiding preparation before the next session. I list intellection and decision together since decision is the product of intellection. In this first round of teaching I develop the outline of the IDEAS diagram shown in Table 2.

Early Development of IDEAS Diagram

Intellection/Decision	Emotion
control: 99% + *Romans 12:2*	
Situation	Action
control: none to some; indirect	control: a lot

Table 2

First I quote one or two of the client's comments about unpleasant feelings and write the word *emotions* (or *feelings*) on the pad with some of the client's emotions beneath it. Then I ask, "Where do feelings come from?" The most common first answer is to project the blame on other persons or events in the situation. I write down "situations."

"Where else might feelings come from?" Get the three sources (intellection, actions, situations), accepting the counselee's terminology.

This is the Socratic teaching style: a series of questions that lead the client through a logical sequence toward a predetermined end. We are *not* determining the answers, but we are insisting that certain questions be faced. The purpose is to help the client unravel the destructive chain of I-D-E-A-S.

The process continues with more questions, often in the sequence shown here. The answers are in parentheses.

"What kinds of feelings are there?" (Pleasant and unpleasant; physical and emotional.) I often just mention this in passing; it's not an important teaching point.

"What are the situations that lead to these feelings?"

"What affects situations?" (Our actions, the actions of others, environmental influences such as the economy, disease, accidents.)

"Over which of these three—thoughts, actions, situations—do we have the greatest amount of control?" (Thoughts.)

"The least?" (Situations.) I write, beside the words: *thoughts*, 99%+; *actions*, a lot; *situations*, none to some, and indirect (meaning that control is indirect). These two questions are particularly important because they are the groundwork for the assumptions that follow.

I conclude this portion of the process by asking for agreement to this summary of assumptions: a. We don't have much control over situations, but we have almost complete control over what we think. b. How we think affects how we feel. c. If we want to feel better, the first place to make changes is where we have greatest control: thoughts. This is down to earth and logical to them, and is also a good time to mention Romans 12:2 and point out that the Bible is not only true but practical for the nitty-grittys of life.

2. *Gather information.* Now I choose a situation to work on. Usually I will not have brought up the IDEAS method until I have heard a situation that lends itself clearly to analysis by this process and I think the client is receptive. We can start anywhere, but it's usually easiest to start with a situation and move chronologically.

"When that happened, how did you feel?" I write down the answer. Then, questions such as: "What came next? What were you thinking during this time? What else was going on?" As I gather items I write them in the quadrant where they belong.

3. *Organize and interpret.* Now I will number the items in chronological sequence. If I wish to leave room for parts of the sequence that preceded the first item I know about now, I number the first item "20" so we can work backward in sequence if we want to.

Include all the important intellections you can. You won't know all the important ones; the diagram will help you find them. Here you will do some strategic teaching as you help the counselee discover important beliefs and learn how they lead to emotions or actions that are beneficial or destructive.

Some of the beliefs you find will prove to be bogus, and therefore, they will reveal themselves as a major contributor to the disruption. Whatever you call these—irrational thinking, erroneous beliefs, stinkin' thinkin'—it is very helpful to find them. It is not much fun, but very helpful: beneficial bad news.

Help persons understand how useful it is to discover their irrational beliefs. Affirm them vigorously for each discovery. Look for conflicts between belief and action. When a person acts in violation of belief it is as though the mind is going west and the body is going east. This puts tremendous strain on the entire system. It is as though a civil war is going on and this person is the battlefield. No wonder there is pain! When belief calls for action and the person does not act, a similar conflict exists. The mind says "go west" and the body doesn't move. This is not quite as painful, but still debilitating.

To understand the relationships among the components usually proves a highly motivating factor for counselees and takes the mystery out of the emotional state they are in. An example from a counseling session with Bram illustrates this. Here is the dialogue from part of a session.

54. Bram: I might as well give up. I'm not good enough for my family.
55. Pastor: You know that I disagree with that, but tell me what's behind such strong statements.

56. Bram: Well, I blew up again. At my daughter. And over nothing.

57. Pastor: Let's talk about it, and learn from it.

58. Bram: She didn't clean out the kitty litter box. I've told her and told her and told her, but she doesn't do it. I reminded her this morning, but there it was tonight, she hadn't cleaned it. Then I yelled at her about it.

59. Pastor: How did you feel, *before* you yelled at her?

60. Bram: Mad. Boy, was I *mad*!

61. Pastor: It would be helpful to you to know *why* you were so angry. Do you remember what you were thinking, *before* you yelled at her?

62. Bram: Yeah. I was thinking, she isn't ever going to do this right.

63. Pastor: I suppose it might seem to you that no matter how you try to teach about this, the message isn't getting through. If so, that would be discouraging for you.

64. Bram: Yeah.

65. Pastor: So that's frustrating for you, and maybe, just maybe, it might even seem like a slap in the face to you because it seems to you like you're not getting the amount of respect from her that you deserve.

66. Bram: Yeah! I remember thinking, *If they respected me, even a little bit, they would cooperate better than this.*

67. Pastor: So you felt put down, which is very painful. Even so, your reaction was out of proportion, which makes me wonder what your day was like before you got home.

68. Bram: It was kind of a tough day. I goofed up an order, so that was on my mind. I was all thumbs all day. I guess my brain was a thumb, too!

69. Pastor: You had a lot of frustration all day long?

70. Bram: I worried a lot about my mistake.

71. Pastor: What were some of your *thoughts*?

72. Bram: That I don't do my work very well anymore, and if I keep making mistakes like this I could lose my job.

73. Pastor: That would be a lot to worry about if it were true. Are you *sure* that it is true?

74. Bram: You know how I am; how I can make a mountain out of a molehill.

75. Pastor: (chuckles) You've been listening in here, haven't you!

76. Bram: I remember that we talked about how it has always been hard for me to trust people. Do you suppose that the trouble I have trusting people is part of what went wrong today?

77. Pastor: We have quite a few pieces of the puzzle on the table right now. Let's see if we can put them together and get the answer to your question.

During the conversation the pastor had taken notes in the IDEAS pattern. The pastor showed this to Bram and put the items in sequence, beginning with item 20, as shown in Table 3. This sequence is much different than the sequence in which Bram presented it.

IDEAS Diagram: Bram

Intellection/Decision	Emotion
18. people can't be trusted	19. anxiety
23. I don't do my work well	26. anxiety about work
25. I could lose my job	29. worthlessness, anger
28. If they respected me . . .	32. fear, anger
31. now I've done it!	

Situation	Actions
21. customer returned wrong part	20. gave customer wrong part
24. learned that customer complained to the boss	22. made exchange
27. dirty kitty litter box	30. yelled at daughter

Table 3

The pastor asked Bram if he *really* believed the statements listed under intellection/decision. Bram decided that he did not, but realized that he was allowing them to affect him as though they were true. The pastor then added items 18 and 19, information gathered in other sessions, and directed the discussion to the roots of Bram's anxiety. The pastor showed Bram the connections between his beliefs during childhood and now, and taught Bram how those old patterns could change.

Now, let's add another element in the system. Orthodox Christianity teaches that there are absolutes that govern belief and behavior: truth. All truth comes from God as part of his creation, given to us as an expression of his love, and it is possible for us to know that portion of truth that is essential to our living with contentment in this world.

Some of your counselee's problems may result from conflicts between belief or action and truth. Searching for those discrepancies is a natural and essential part of Christian counseling. We do this, not to condemn or to punish people, but as an expression of our own love—we want persons to remove every burden that encumbers them in their journey of life. You can affirm individuals for facing these conflicts and offer them the good news that God is ready to forgive and help them overcome belief or behavior that distances them from God.

IDEAS Diagram: Example of Conflicts

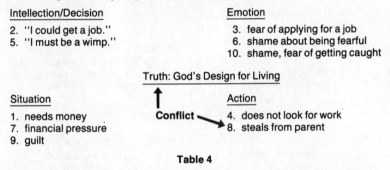

This is a high-school-age boy in a Christian family.

Intellection/Decision	Emotion
2. "I could get a job."	3. fear of applying for a job
5. "I must be a wimp."	6. shame about being fearful
	10. shame, fear of getting caught

Truth: God's Design for Living

Situation		Action
1. needs money	**Conflict**	4. does not look for work
7. financial pressure		8. steals from parent
9. guilt		

Table 4

I often highlight these conflicts on the diagram. See Table 4 for a simple example. The boy needs money (1), knows he could get a job (2), and so on. Follow the chain of development. After organizing the diagram, the counselor can easily show where some of the pain comes from (6 follows 4 and 5; 10 follows 8 and 9), which leads naturally to considering alternatives.

4. *Build a plan.* Now you have found where many of the problems start. You have taught this to the counselee. Next, you develop a plan he or she can follow to move from distress to contentment.

Knowing there is a plan boosts people's hopes. They can see that they have two changes (or five or whatever) to make and, even though they know that it may not be easy to make the changes, there is great comfort in having a plan. This increases their confidence in the counselor, and it supports them in the hard work of changing beliefs or behaviors to know why the efforts should pay off in a better situation and better feelings.

Table 5 shows how the counselor helped the boy look at alternatives to stealing money from his parents. The new information was simply added to Table 4, so the counselor used letters to show the new pattern. It is not a "Pollyanna" plan that assumes full success; the actions are partially successful, but bring emotional rewards. Notice the destructive thoughts and painful feelings that are bypassed with the plan.

IDEAS: Diagram: Building a Plan

Same high-school-age boy as in Table 4.

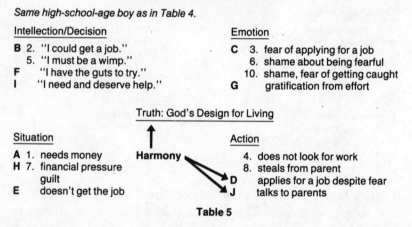

Intellection/Decision

B 2. "I could get a job."
  5. "I must be a wimp."
F   "I have the guts to try."
I   "I need and deserve help."

Emotion

C 3. fear of applying for a job
  6. shame about being fearful
 10. shame, fear of getting caught
G   gratification from effort

Truth: God's Design for Living

Situation

A 1. needs money
H 7. financial pressure
     guilt
E   doesn't get the job

Harmony

Action

 4. does not look for work
 8. steals from parent
D   applies for a job despite fear
J   talks to parents

Table 5

5. *Implement the plan.* The client follows the plan. With a plan, goals for behavioral change can be clearly defined and attainable, including monitoring and eliminating destructive mental habits. This makes it easy to agree on goals for change between sessions and to hold the client accountable.

Clients can work out more diagrams on their own time, and that is good, for it speeds up the counseling process. I have had excellent cooperation with this as a homework assignment. The quality of understanding that clients have gained and the increase in commitment to change have been remarkable.

CHAPTER NINE

COUNSELING AND THE PROBLEM: TURN

WILL THE COUNSELEE CHOOSE HEALING AND LIFE or remain in the grip of the disorder? The moment of truth approaches when his or her freedom will be used for benefit or for destruction.

STAGE 5: TURN TOWARD HEALTH

Growth is a choice. Those who escape self-control disorders do so because they choose to. They *decide* to begin living differently. A few days ago a man told me, "When I quit smoking I *decided* I just had to quit, so I did. I never could have done it except that I *decided* I was going to." He didn't try to make it sound easy, which it wasn't, but he wanted to emphasize the importance of decision.

If we are to act differently, we must decide to. Christianity makes it inescapably clear that the direction we turn is within our control. The word *turn* is used hundreds of times between Genesis and Revelation, and around that word is written the history of humanity. The Israelites turned away from God (Exod. 32:8, 1 Sam. 12:21), back (2 Chron. 19:4), and away again (Jer. 2:29, 8:5). Some people turned away from Jesus in his presence (Luke 4:28–30) and others turned toward him (Luke 6:17–19).

God's judgment on those who turn away is clear (Deut. 31:18, 2 Chron. 7:19), but so is his invitation to turn toward our inheritance (Deut. 30:9, 10; Acts 14:14–17). Our thematic verse, Isaiah 6:10, with its clear invitation to turn so we may be healed, is quoted in the New Testament three times (Matt. 13:15; John 12:40, and Acts 28:27).

Stage 5 is decision time. As counselors we must call our counselees/friends to "choose for yourselves this day whom you will serve" (Josh. 24:15). The invitation must be clear.

Up to this point we have asked the individual for commitment only to the counseling process; now we ask for commitment to change in behavior. The processes in the first four stages have, for the most part, been invitational; now we may push.

Counselor Process: Show Client Responsibility Clearly

We have hoped that by considering the facts the client will recognize personal responsibility for the disorder and its solution. We may have used the IDEAS diagram to teach this and we may have prayed for the Holy Spirit to instruct this person through us and directly.

We have done all we have known to "connect" lovingly with the person, to unravel the past, and to persuade that there is a better way. That is all we can do unless the counselee opts for change; it is all that God asks of us.

Counselee Input: Accept Responsibility for Problem

Disordered persons rarely change until they admit that they are the ones who have acted and thought destructively and recognize that they have a choice about it. They may not be responsible for conditions that encouraged the disorder to begin, but they must accept responsibility for having chosen to continue it. They must accept responsibility for the process of change. They must "own" the problem.

Owning the problem—admitting that they cause the costs— is the single most important element in the change of a disorder of self-control. Self-help organizations such as Alcoholics Anonymous insist that participants admit at the outset that they are powerless to control their problem. Psychology is showing a renewal of interest in personal volition in behavior. For more information on the importance of personal responsibility, read books by Lawrence Crabb and William Glasser.[1]

Illustration from Bram

78. Bram has just described an incident of a few days ago in which he was explosive and adds: "They shouldn't expect me to be able to control myself perfectly all the time. Sometimes a man does something and he just can't help it."
79. Pastor: What does that mean to you?
80. Bram: What it means is that since I don't know why I did it, they shouldn't hassle me about it. They can hassle me about the parts of life I have control over, but not this; this isn't fair.
81. Pastor: I agree that no one should expect you to be perfect all the time, but I disagree with the last thing you said. If I understand you right, you are saying that this is beyond your control. Well, there is some good news for you and that good news is that you *can* have self-control that you don't have now. I would like for us to use our time together to help you get the self-control you don't have now. What would *you* like?

The pastor uses questions (79, 81) to keep Bram actively involved. Question 79 is open-ended and elicits some information the pastor disagrees with. In 81, the pastor confronts with other information, offers hope, and uses a very specific question meant to move Bram toward action.

Counselee Input: Accept Responsibility for Change

The person immersed in the problem says, "I don't have a problem. My only problem is with the people who keep telling me I have a problem." It's a great leap forward to the point of saying, "Yes, I have a problem." The process of rebuilding begins when the client says, "I will do whatever it takes to clean up my act and live right."

One of the tasks of counseling is to bring the person to a point of decision. We want the client to move from acceptance of the disordered behavior to consideration of alternatives, to the point that the tug of war between the disordered pattern and a new pattern is very strong—and eventually for disgust and despair over the disordered pattern to grow and the alternative to become more appealing.

When persons believe they didn't cause a problem, they usually believe they can't change it. So, admission of responsibility for the problem comes first. Before change begins, you will probably have to hear them say, "I have a problem and I am ready to do something about it." You can affirm their courage and honesty, and offer hope that they can make the changes.

82. Pastor: Are you saying, then, that you'll do the things that you can do to change?

83. Bram: If Glenda does her part.

84. Pastor: She says she will, which allows you to concentrate on your part.

85. Bram: What is she going to do?

86. Pastor: That's not as important right now as what *you* will do. Will you do *your* part?

87. Bram: But I'm not the only one with a problem.

88. Pastor: You're right! But, do you agree that *part* of the responsibility for the problem rests with you?

89. Bram: Yeah.

90. Pastor: And, aren't you the only one who can change *your* part of the problem?

91. Bram: Yeah.

92. Pastor: Then where do we go from here?

93. Bram: Well . . . I guess I do what I have to do.

94. Pastor: Yes! Terrific, because doing what is yours to do will be good for you. One thing that I believe would be helpful to you is to read this book during the next week. Will you do that?

95. Bram: (Reaches for book.)

96. Pastor: Great! How much would you read in the next week?

97. Bram: All of it.

98. Pastor: Fantastic!

The pastor expresses confidence in Glenda (84), refuses to follow Bram's sidestepping (84, 86), and gently but persistently nudges Bram to a decision (88–96) for which he affirms Bram (96, 98).

Counselor Process: Teach Coping Skills

Coping skills help a person minimize the problem while the main counseling work of locating and resolving the root problems is going on. *As valuable as coping skills are in the early part of counseling, they are no substitute for resolving the root conditions of the disorder!*

There are six appendixes at the end of the book that can help clients cope with their disorders. They are designed to be copied and, with minimal instruction, given to the client as "homework." For more techniques, I suggest that the counselor consult recommended books.[2]

Counselee Input: Learn and Use Coping Skills

Slowing down the disorder with "cease fire" and coping methods proves to the counselee that the problem can get better. That is emotionally rewarding and builds motivation to learn more and work harder. With disorders of self-control there often is conflict with friends and family members who are affected by the counselee's lack of self-control. When these persons see the counselee taking steps to resolve the disorder, they may reduce their condemnation of him or her. This is another reward.

Some of the methods may seem a little silly at first. That's okay. What's a trifling amount of embarrassment compared to the pain of the problem? If the counselor has been credible in the past and has developed a good relationship, the individual will try new things although they require a bit of daring or discipline. Although the coping methods may give only temporary relief of symptoms, they can be a step in the path to health.

Illustration from Bram

99. Pastor: In the past, when you've felt yourself getting angry, what has helped you control yourself?
100. Bram: If I can, I get away from whatever is bothering me. Sometimes that's only a minute, but it helps.
101. Pastor: Good! What else?
102. Bram: I put my mind on other things. Happier things.
103. Pastor: Good! Do you ever pray for self-control?
104. Bram: I have done that.
105. Pastor: And . . . ?
106. Bram: I think that has helped.
107. Pastor: I'm *sure* it has. This is good, Bram. You have found three ways to cope with the situation in the heat of the battle: getting away, putting your mind on other things, and prayer. I'm glad these methods have been helpful to you. I call these "first aid" methods because they bring some quick relief during the crisis. But, first aid may not be enough. That's the case for you now. We need to find the *source* of the problems and fix it at that point. In the meantime, it will be important for you to keep your anger under control as best you can. Here is a list of "first aid" methods for coping with anger. (See Appendix 1.) Let's go over these quickly just to clarify what they are. In this list, you may find another approach or two you can use in addition to the methods you just mentioned.

Comments: The pastor asks Bram what he has done in the past (99). This shows respect (by recognizing that Bram has learned through experience) and saves time. Affirmation is given (101, 103, 107) and teaching begins (107).

CHAPTER TEN

COUNSELING AND THE PROBLEM: BE HEALED

WHEN YOU BEGIN COUNSELING, expect to see God at work! I know of no greater thrill than to be with persons when God is repairing and improving their lives. The most exciting part of the process is during Stage 6.

STAGE 6: BE HEALED

"I have come that you might have life and have it to the full," Jesus said (John 10:10). God is the Creator of life and health! It pleases him to calm the turbulence of our confusion, heal wounds that have been inflicted upon us, and fill empty places that were meant to be filled by parental love and companionship. He does not change the historical facts of our lives, but frees us from their consequences.

He offers us a way out of the pits we have been thrown into, pulls out the thorns we have fallen upon, and lifts the bags of sand we have picked up along the way.

Counselor Process: Guide the Counselee to
Resolution of Root Problems

When working with Christian clients the counselor has more ways to help than when working with non-Christian clients. We can pray with a client for discernment and courage in restitution or reconciliation. We can ask God to heal painful memories or fill deficits of parental love. We can apply the authority of Scripture to puzzling situations. Best of all, we can experience the Holy Spirit's nurture and guidance through every part of the counseling process!

Here is a summary of how persons reach resolution of six root problems. Part Two of this book presents a case study of each, with more suggestions about the counseling process.

1. *Sinful nature.* The problem is our alienation from God. The solution is salvation—accepting his offer of reconciliation, made possible by the death and resurrection of Jesus Christ. Harmony with God is necessary in order to have full measure of quality of life. Counseling without attention to the need for salvation is incomplete; teaching people that they can reach maturity without dealing with sin is foolish and cruel.

2. *Physiological disadvantages.* Some physical problems are healed.[1] I am enthusiastic about God's love to us and the frequency with which he expresses his love through direct intervention. When I am involved with people in counseling we often pray for God to heal.

Healing is best sought through mainstream resources of the congregation: a healing service, in conjunction with communion, with the participation of the pastor and elders or deacons.[2] When I pray with a client about physical healing it is generally for direction about how to seek healing and it is in support of the congregation's corporate healing ministry.

Relief may come through the healing professions. God has equipped humans to unfold many of the mysteries of our world. From these efforts we have medicine, therapies for disorders of speech or learning, support groups for families affected by birth defects or diseases, and many other means of reducing the distress. It is not only proper for Christians to use these resources; to reject them may be a repudiation of God's grace.

Sometimes the disability remains, but the person learns to cope with it. From my study window I can see Long's Peak, 14,256 feet above sea level, towering above other rugged peaks in Rocky Mountain National Park. Climbing it is a rigorous eighteen-mile hike that requires excellent conditioning and leaving the trail head several hours before sunrise. Many people who try to climb it give up before the summit; most people don't try.

Mike Smithson is a ranger-naturalist at Rocky Mountain. During college a logging accident left his legs paralyzed. Not an office type, he covers his jurisdiction by car and an "off-the-road" wheelchair. He has also built a low seat with a peg on the bottom that he straps on to move himself, by hands and seat, over rocks and up steep inclines. Last summer Mike climbed Long's Peak. Mike Smithson copes.

God does not always heal bodies, but he will always heal life. For some persons, learning to cope with conditions that won't change is part of the healing process.

We will not ask people to deny their frustration. We will not suggest that they stifle thoughts and emotions. We propose that they approach life in a new way, allowing the blood of Christ's atonement to reconstruct their responses to painful circumstances. I am reminded of a magic trick I did as a child. A glass of "water" poured into another glass turned red, and then, poured into a third glass, turned clear again. This is how God's cleansing of circumstances works. We do not pretend that the "bloody situation" is not there, but the power of Christ transforms it, makes it transparent, so we have no fear that something dangerous is within.

3. and 4. *Deficits and wounds.* The counselor may need to help clients discover sins committed against persons who have hurt them (or failed to nurture them). We are usually pretty good at hiding these from ourselves. Time and again I have seen healing come to a person *only after* confession and repentance before God of sins against others who have hurt them.

Often, individuals are unaware of their retaliatory acts and attitudes. I begin by teaching that it "just may be possible that these exist" and use an example or two from my own life to illustrate how we may retaliate through sneaky means, to demonstrate candor, and to praise God for healing I have received.

Forgiving seems commonly to be the necessary second step. It means giving up all claim upon one who has hurt you, including letting go of the emotional consequences of the hurt. Forgiving is contrary to our culture which views it as weakness and prefers to seek revenge. Forgiving models God's mercy to us; it frees us from bondage under resentment and liberates us to grow, mature, and enter productive service. The case in chapter 15 illustrates how quickly and radically forgiving can improve a person's life.

Deficits, the empty places in a person's life that result from what parents (or other important persons) didn't provide, may be filled by God's direct intervention. It's like this: imagine that we are building a wooden chest and that one of the boards has a knothole in it. The red-brown resinous knot has fallen out, leaving a hole and weakening the board. We can fill that hole with epoxy patching material, sand it smooth, paint it, and that board will be as beautiful and as strong as a board that grew with straight grain and no knots. A person who did not know the history of that board would never guess that it had once been defective.

This illustrates God's healing. He fills empty places in people, rebuilding them so they are as strong, beautiful, and functional as if they had grown up under ideal conditions.

5. *Discrepancies.* Since these are the result of untruth, they are corrected by displacing untruth with truth. "You were taught," Paul writes the Ephesians, "with regard to your former way of life, to put off your old self, which is being corrupted by its deceitful desires; to be made new in the attitude of your minds; and to put on the new self, created to be like God in true righteousness and holiness" (Eph. 4:22–24). How?

First, break destructive habits. *Put off the old,* Paul says—extinguish the unhealthy behavior. Strategies to assist this are described in Appendixes 2 and 4. Then, adopt Christlike patterns. *Put on the new,* Paul says—learn to live right. Churches can do this with excellence because the mechanisms for bringing people to the healing power of Christ are in place: personal discipleship, experiences of worship, education, fellowship, and other means described in chapter 20.

6. *Consequences of sins.* The counselor will help the client evaluate these. The remedies for physiological consequences are the same as listed above for physiological disadvantages. The remedy for guilt is confession and repentance, and receiving God's forgiveness. The remedy for shame is to *accept* God's forgiveness. This is in addition to receiving forgiveness and is illustrated in chapter 16. Relational consequences are remedied through reconciliation (when possible) and learning the Christ-style of relationship. These changes are much more likely to occur after guilt and shame have been relieved.

Illustration from Bram

The primary root problems for Bram were the wounds from his father's harsh behavior and the deficits of affection not received from his parents. These problems had led to his deferential and task-oriented approach to other people. Bram's own explosiveness had left consequences that needed relational healing, which could come only after his "heart" had been mended.

The pastor and Bram prayed together for God's healing. As they did this, session by session, Bram became aware of the intense anger he had toward his parents. He prayed, repenting of his sins of resentment. As he relinquished his bitterness about incidents he remembered, new memories surfaced. He dealt with those the same way.

The result was more memories and less pain. He became more relaxed, trusting, and free in the give-and-take of family life. He was on his way!

Counselor Process: Foster the Fulfillment of Needs

The counselor wants to be sure clients are able to have their needs met. It surprises some that God wants them to have their needs met, as stated in Philippians 4:19, "God will meet all your needs according to his glorious riches in Christ Jesus." It's okay to want your needs met.

Some people think they *need* their *wants* met. In that case the counselor will help them shift from the never-ending frustration of human greed to the satisfaction of living within God's priorities.

The Lord knows what we need (Matt. 6:32) and we do not need to worry (Luke 12:22-34). But we are also told, "Ask and it will be given to you; seek and you will find; knock and the door will be opened to you" (Luke 11:9). Ask, seek, knock. The counselor may be called upon to teach the skills of asking, direct the seeking, or be with counselees during the knocking.

Helping people learn how to fulfill their needs is common-sense counseling: encouraging people to find and use community resources; using the congregation's networks to find jobs, housing, used furniture, baby-sitters, or carpools; finding or creating opportunities for basic education in life skills such as personal finance or job hunting; developing Christian education and worship that makes a difference Monday through Saturday. In this part of counseling lay counselors are often more effective than professionals.

CHAPTER ELEVEN

WHAT TO DO WHEN COUNSELING IS NOT WANTED

THE DAY I BEGAN WRITING THIS CHAPTER my son Dan and I started building a small privacy fence to hide the garbage cans and firewood beside the garage. We bought lumber and rented a two-man, gasoline-powered post-hole digger.

It was a hot August day. The sun blazed down on us and even though the heavy machine growled steadily through the dry, gravelly soil it was hard work. Now, Dan and I come from a long line of skinny guys and we don't look like guys who dig post holes, even with a machine, so we got very tired. Quickly.

Then, at high noon, digging the third hole, the auger chewed into a streak of moist bentonite, which is a heavy, gummy clay that will grab anything it touches and hang on to it like a hungry beagle on a ham bone. If there is a soil type that is totally depraved, it is bentonite. Don't dig holes in wet bentonite!

Our auger was thirty inches deep when the engine stalled, the auger welded into the world with stubborn bentonite. We restarted the engine and we lifted, we heaved and ho'd, and we grunted and strained—and the obstinate bentonite just pulled back in the other direction. There was no way we were going to win a tug of war with Mother Earth!

So we dug clay out with our fingers and with a small gardening claw, we used two-by-fours to pry upward on the machine, and it took us forty-five sweaty, painful minutes to get that machine out of the grip of the bentonite. We were exhausted! I was sure I was about to have a heart attack but going to the intensive care unit appealed to me more than digging another hole, so it didn't matter! We both dearly wanted to quit—we wanted shade and lunch and rest, sweet rest. We wanted to quit but we needed one more hole. What did we do? We dug the hole. Why?

ACTIONS FOLLOW MOTIVATION

We dug the hole because we were motivated. What were our motivations? As usual, there were several: to not admit defeat, to save forty dollars by not having to rent the machine another day, to have the satisfaction of finishing the job, to have the satisfaction of persistence in the face of difficulty (for me—to model persistence to Dan). And when I took the machine back and the clerk said, "How did it go?" I wanted to be able to toss back a casual, "Oh, no sweat. Nothing to it. Punched a few holes into some bentonite. You've heard how tough that can be! But, heh heh heh, it was no match for *us*!"

What was the level of maturity of our motivations? I don't think any of them were immature, although the motivation that springs from anger and says "I'm not going to let that stupid bentonite beat me" is at the primitive end of the maturity scale! What counted was that the motivations for doing what we *needed* outweighed, to the satisfaction of our wills, the motivations for doing what we *wanted*. This is a contest you wage in your own life; this is a contest your clients bring with them.

Some motivators are primarily emotional, others are primarily rational. Being in a contest with the clay—rallying strength to win a tug of war with Opponent Bentonite—is emotional! It is rational to say "if we dig out the clay as far as we can reach maybe we can start the engine and lift up some more and we can dig that out. That won't be too hard. We'll rest up and get the auger out and then we can dig the other hole and move along with what we started."

Some motivators are toward a positive: the fence will look great when it's finished, we'll have lunch as soon as we finish this hole, we'll have more room in the garage with the cans outside. Others are away from a negative: it's going to cost another forty dollars if we have to rent the digger another day, the pile of lumber is going to be sitting there until we get the holes dug, we expected to dig these four holes and I just don't want to fail at it!

Both types are legitimate and can work together like two horses in a team. The motivators toward positives and those away from negatives are usually headed in the same direction, so they combine in force.

Everyone Is Always Motivated

Everyone is motivated. If a person acts, he or she is motivated. This includes your counselees who frustrated you because when you wanted them to "go south" they "went north," or did not move at all. They were motivated, even if you didn't understand what they wanted or why. Whether motivators exist is not a question. They do.

Persons' responses to counseling are related to their level of motivation for change. Your method of counseling is related to your estimate of their motivation. You will use a different approach with someone who is highly motivated than with one who is resistant to change.

SIGNS OF MOTIVATION IN COUNSELING

Some people are motivated to constructive living. Persons who are motivated believe that if they change to a new pattern of living they will get more of their needs met than if they continue the present pattern. The belief will be expressed in behavior the counselor can observe. People who have high levels of motivation:

- *own the problem.* They admit, credibly, having a problem. They are in counseling at their own initiative; outside pressure may exist but is not needed.
- *work with the process.* They volunteer relevant, sensitive, personal information even when that is difficult. They willingly give appropriate effort such as: driving a distance to come to counseling, paying a baby-sitter, paying for counseling, taking time off work at personal expense, or giving diligent attention to homework assignments.
- *set goals.* They identify how they want things to be different. The goals are concrete, realistic, and they have subgoals that systematically lead to the primary goal.

Signs of Low Motivation

Counselees who are not motivated for change believe—perhaps stubbornly and in the face of overwhelming evidence—that the present pattern of living will work at least as well or better than any other pattern.[1] Those who have low levels of motivation:

- *reject responsibility.* If they recognize a problem, they put the blame on circumstances or other people.
- *give little effort.* They are tardy or skip appointments, offering flimsy excuses. They do not follow through with homework assignments or are unreliable in other ways.
- *have no goals.* Or, they reject goals they have previously agreed to, deflect the counselor's efforts to help them set goals, or disagree with the counselor's interpretation of goals that have been set.

Reasons Motivation May Be Low

Counselees may not be motivated for a constructive change of their self-control disorders.[2] There are several kinds of problems.

1. *Defect of problem ownership.* If change is to be permanent, the motivation for change must be within the individual. Sometimes family and friends are motivated for the person to change, but he or she is not. Change that comes from pressure put on the person by others is usually nothing more than conformity. "I went along with what she wanted just to get her off my back."

2. *Defect of world view.* My impulses would have me dash frantically from urge to urge. That's tyranny!

Culture bombards me with demands; it would have me make down payments on seven cars and a truck and rush from there to the "Midnight Madness Sale" at Honest Arnold's Electronics World to buy a TV set with a screen too big to fit in my house. That's tyranny!

Christianity answers the conflict between what we need and what we want. Wanting what God wants for us provides everything we need. Perfectly. Christianity leads us away from what culture wants us to want, to what God wants us to be. When we are who God wants us to be our needs are met. Perfectly.

Culture shock? The shock does not come from what culture is doing, but from trying to do what it asks of us. Clients may have motivation for constructive change, but culture will encourage patterns that are contrary to change. Christianity gives us a way to say no.

3. *Defect of type.* Identifying the motivators is quite another matter. People often are not sure of their own motivations. How often have you heard someone say, "I don't know why I did such a thing"? One of the counselor's tasks, and joys, is helping clients identify the emotions and beliefs that motivate their behavior. After the counselor helps the client identify motivators that lead away from health and maturity, the client must refute them.

People will trade something valuable for something more valuable to them, or for the hope of getting something more valuable. But, unless handicapped by a disorder in thought process, people do not give up something valuable for nothing. When behavior changes, the person's priorities have changed. The one safe set of priorities for us is God's set of priorities because, as I quoted Paul earlier, "The mind controlled by the Spirit is life and peace" (Rom. 8:6).

People pursue behavior that makes sense to them, even though it is not valid by God's principles. Many reasons can be given for why people may reject God's patterns:

a. They may misunderstand the nature of God. They may have been misled by theology that presents God as weak, or overwhelmed and out of control, as dead or dying, or as aloof and uncaring. They need to know that God is "alive and well," and that he offers us personal friendship and nurture.

b. They may perceive God as punitive, a viewpoint often seen in the counseling room. This may result from teaching at church that emphasized God's wrath to the exclusion of his love, or from painful experience with a punitive earthly father. The good news of the gospel fixes that when people give it a chance. *If* they give it a chance.

c. They may believe that Christian living is ungratifying. This unfortunate impression may come from experience with earnest Christians who are stuffy. I recall, with mixed feelings, a woman in her midtwenties who attended a workshop I held several years ago. She described herself as "an Army brat who grew up all over the country." About half the twenty people in the workshop identified themselves as Christian; she did not. As we closed the four days of training she told the group, "This is the first time in my life I have been with Christians who are fun to be with."

d. They may have had bad experiences with hypocrites. A man once said to me, "The biggest thing keeping me from being a Christian is _____." He named one of my church's elders. That's not a good reason, but it was good enough for him.

e. They may be rebelling. The disorder may be the "rope" in a tug of war with God or with another person.

INCREASING A PERSON'S MOTIVATION

You may be able to create some conditions that will increase the counselee's motivation. Consider these possibilities:

1. *Conviction by the Holy Spirit.* Pray for him or her. Ask God to develop, through the work of the Holy Spirit, the

person's hunger for a better life, and for you and the client to understand the problems and to have faith that change is worthwhile and is possible. God wants health and happiness for the person as much as you do.

2. *Your relationship with the person.* If the way you live is attractive to the counselee—if it shows that you are getting your needs met—it increases your influence with him or her. Here, you are benefiting from your investment in building trust and rapport.

3. *The person's relationship with other valued persons.* It may be possible to enlist the support of friends or family members as constructive influences—to confront or encourage. Two cautions: (a) They may already have tried their best; (b) the need for confidentiality may prevent you from talking to the person you need most as an ally in the case.

4. *Clear goals set by the person.* Ask (insist if you must) that the person set at least one behavioral goal to reach before the next appointment. Accept small goals if they are worthy. The internal rewards—sense of accomplishment, confidence, proper pride—increase the likelihood of setting and reaching the next goal.

5. *External pressure.* "Hitting bottom" is painful: shame and despair can be intense, a person may feel worthless and without hope. It can be a dangerous time and must never be taken lightly. Sometimes, however, it is appropriate to increase pressure on the counselee so he or she hits bottom.

This may be done by expecting people to perform before they get something pleasant. Parents do this when they say, "You can't have the ice cream unless you eat your lima beans." If you have ever been through that with a child, multiply the difficulty by a hundred or more to estimate what you are in for with an adult who has a disorder of self-control! But, this is an approach that you may need to use. The better the relationship with the person, the higher the chances that this will be helpful.

This might be done letting the person take the consequences of his or her behavior. For example, to let an alcoholic stay in jail the full period of time or to allow repossession of the car. When these strong actions are taken one must show the individual as clearly as possible that these are actions of love. This is difficult for the person to see, of course.

6. *A cocounselor with "been there" authority.* If the person's counselor or friend has "been there" it is more difficult for the person to reject suggestions or confrontations. That is why many of the self-help groups such as Alcoholics Anonymous are so effective. Consider referring the person to such a group or counselor, or ask someone who has life experience with the disorder to join you as a cocounselor. This person need not be a professional counselor.

Do not discount what you can accomplish even though you have not "been there." Many years ago, during my training, I was asked to lead a counseling group of alcoholics, most of whom were homeless men. They treated me charitably, but with visible skepticism. "Are you an alcoholic?" they asked. "No." "Have you ever had the d.t.'s?" "No." If they had chosen to, they could have ignored my observations, beliefs, or confrontations by telling themselves that because I hadn't "been there" I couldn't know anything.

That is one of the experiences that taught me the power of relationship, for as my relationship with them developed I earned credibility with them and had some constructive influence. It is likely to take longer if you haven't "been there," but you will still be able to help the client.

7. *Eliminating rescuers and cheerleaders.* Rescuers are those friends and family who rush in to "pull the person out of the fire"; for example, the parent who pays a son's college tuition after the son squanders his salary from a summer job instead of saving it for tuition as had been agreed. A cheerleader is someone who benefits from the person's disorder, and thus gives encouragement and support to it; for example, a spouse who smokes and who encourages the other partner's overeating. (When this activity disrupts the counseling process, I call it sabotage. See discussion in chapter 12.)

8. *Intellectual consistency.* A person may hold to valid principles but act in violation of them. If this person puts a high value on intellectual consistency, pointing out this dichotomy and calling for internal consistency may get the ball rolling.

For example, a counselor said to Marc, "You told me week before last, last week, and again today that you believe it is wrong for you to continue doing that, yet you continue. What *do* you believe?" Because Marc valued consistency, this confrontation was enough.

We can even confront ourselves. A courageous and intellectually honest pastor mentally confronted himself about his poor stewardship of time as he stood preaching to his congregation about the stewardship of money.

TYPES OF RATIONALIZATIONS

There are as many ways to avoid counseling as there are ways to need it. The more intelligent and creative the client, the more reasonable the excuses will sound. Every counselor is sure to hear many of these patterns:

1. *False altruism.*

"My counseling is hurting (counselee names someone) because . . . ."

"I don't have time to do things for them."

"We can't afford it."

"They like me better the way I am than if I were to change."

"It upsets my family that I am changing."

"My husband doesn't like me coming here."

Strategies: Ask that the other people get involved. You might ask the friend or family member to come in as a favor to the counselee, to help you understand him or her better. If these people are interfering, that can be dealt with directly. If this is only the counselee's rationalization, that will be exposed for what it is.

2. *Pessimism about counseling.*

"You don't understand me."

"This just isn't the time for it."

"I'm not ready for it now."

Strategies: My approach usually is to leave the burden of logic with the person by asking why. When there is dissatisfaction with my part of the process I try hard to remedy the situation. This may be an actual defect in my counseling process or it may be a misunderstanding about the roles of counselor and counselee.

3. *Hopelessness about condition.*

"Things can never change."

"My problem is so unusual, no one can help with it."

"I'm incurable. There's no hope for me."

Strategies: I express my conviction that things can change for them because I have seen worse things change for others. I do this quickly. Then I ask them to set a goal for change and we make an action plan that will accomplish it. (If they sabotage that, it shows that the benefits of sabotage were more important to them than the benefits of accomplishing the stated goal. With this, I understand them better.)

4. *Spiritual rationalizations.*

"God is going to do it for me."

"I heard that counseling is evil."

"I don't want to interfere with God's work on me."

Strategies: Define Christian counseling: a combination of friendship and teaching, guided by God's principles and empowered by his love, with the goal of facilitating another person's spiritual, emotional, and relational healing and growth. Teach about the nature of God and his methods of helping us. Experience God's love by praying together.

5. *Excuses to change counselors.*

"My problem isn't psychological, it's medical."

"I heard about a counselor who is closer to my house (or quicker, cheaper, more specialized)."

Strategies: It is important to not become defensive about this. If that is hard for you, don't add to the problem by condemning yourself for the difficulty in being open with them about it. Make it easy for them to tell you dissatisfactions, apprehensions, or displeasures about the counseling with you. Change what you can, but it may be in the person's best interests to be with another counselor. Care whether the person gets better; don't care where it happens.

6. *Flight into health.*

"Everything's okay now."

"I've learned all I need to learn. Now it's just a matter of using what I've learned and I have to do that on my own."

"It's been good, but I don't need it anymore."

Strategies: If I believe that it may be harmful for them to drop out of counseling, I must say so. This must be done with great care because they are on the verge of saying good-bye and I want them to hear what I have to say. I will be very clear in explaining to them why I think they need counseling, with examples and, whenever possible, quoting them to establish the "case."

I wish to make it easy for them to come back for more counseling in the future. For example, I might say, "For many people—probably for *most* people—emotional growth is a gradual thing and they find that they will work hard in counseling for a while and then not need it. Later, something comes up that needs some attention so they are active in counseling again. That's fine. If that's the way it works out for you, please call me. I'm available to be useful to you now if you want that, and I expect to be available to you in the future—whatever's best for you."

7. *Denial.*

"I was wrong about needing counseling. I don't need it."

"I was coming into it for the wrong reasons."

Strategies: Again, I will quote what they have told me about their reasons for needing counseling. I will put the burden on them to demonstrate that things have changed. If I have made careful statements of our problems and objectives for counseling they will be useful to me in this situation.

Summary

We can offer people reasons why they should be motivated toward change, and we can provide opportunity for their small measure of motivation to grow. We may be able to arrange for external pressure to increase, which is sometimes a helpful substitute for internal motivation. But I can't motivate anyone but me, nor can you motivate anyone but you. That is all right. When we have done all that we can, we thank God for having had the opportunity and ask him to bring completion of the work through other means. Rest your heart in that.

CHAPTER TWELVE

WHAT TO DO WHEN FRIENDS OR FAMILY INTERFERE

WHEN PEOPLE BELIEVE THAT BENEFITS from the disorder are greater than the benefits they will get by changing, motivation for change is weak. Chapter 10 discussed this problem and suggested how the counselor can help develop stronger motivation. This chapter discusses a related problem: friends or family members who do not want the person to change. They are motivated by the benefits they receive from the disorder, or by fear of disruption of their own lives if he or she changes.

Often, such people are called enablers because they make it possible for the disorder to continue. I will give them a harsher label, "saboteur," because they disrupt the good work you and your counselee are doing. They may be aware of their resistance and fight in the open, but more often they are not aware of their resistance or of its origin. One of the counselor's tasks is to identify these distractions and help equip the counselee to deal with them. This is sometimes the most challenging part of the counseling process.

MOTIVES OF SABOTEURS

There are many reasons a saboteur may prefer that your counselee not change. Seven motives are illustrated below, and you may encounter even more in your experiences in counseling.

1. *The saboteur wishes to justify a personal problem.* The client is a young man attending a Christian college, and is in counseling for help with obsessive lust.

Client: It's really difficult to get put down for trying to do what's right. My roommate knows I am trying to control my sexual thoughts and behavior but he doesn't help out in the least.

Counselor: Please explain.

Client: I got rid of my porn magazines. He still has his. So he leaves them all over the room—on my chair, on my desk, everywhere.

Counselor: How long has he been doing that?

Client: Uh, you know, I don't think he did that before I decided to get out of it. No, he never did that, before. In fact, he was real protective of them, like he was afraid I would take them.

Counselor: And now it's like an invitation.

Client: Yeah.

Counselor: Do you have any ideas why his style might have changed?

Client: I have a guess. He wants me to get back into it because he's uncomfortable with it himself. If we're both into it, he can justify it to himself by blaming me.

Comments: The client identified the saboteur's motivation. This saved the counselor time and risk. Highly motivated clients are often able to figure these things out as well and as quickly as the counselor. May we counselors rejoice when clients are more skillful than we!

What next? The counselor helped the client recognize anger toward the roommate, retaliation (the silent treatment), and to deal with those issues through confession and repentance. Then the client began praying for his roommate. The counselor coached and rehearsed the client to assertively ask his roommate not to leave his magazines in the open. Because of the change in attitude and approach by the client, the roommate entered counseling to resolve his own problem of obsessive lust.

2. *The saboteur benefits from the client's disorder.* The client is a married man, in counseling because of problems of financial irresponsibility.

Client: My wife says she's 100 percent in favor of the budget we're on, but I don't think she means it.

Counselor: Tell me why you're skeptical.

Client: She keeps showing me things in the newspaper ads, or if we're watching TV she'll oo and ahhh over the new cars. She says things like, "I know this isn't the time to think about it, but won't it be fun when we can afford one of those!" Believe me, I'd like to give her everything she wants, and I try to, but I have to draw the line somewhere or we'll go belly up.

Counselor: How is this affecting you?

Client: It scares me. I think if she keeps chipping away on me like that, I'll just go off on a big spending spree like I've done before.

Counselor: You're afraid of losing control. Anything else?

Client: You mean feelings?

Counselor: Yes. Feelings, or anything else.

Client: It makes me mad. I think that maybe she doesn't care about how I feel or what happens to us financially. She just wants to go on another trip or get something flashy to show off.

Comments: What do *you* think is more important to the client's wife: security or "toys"? Do you suspect that she has histrionic personality traits? The client wants so much to please her that he lets her push him beyond his own weak limits, even to the point that he becomes afraid and angry. Does it not seem reasonable to exercise caution in talking with him about her part in the problem? The counselor, not wanting to turn this person's attention from working on the problem to dislike for the counselor, leads him into discovery instead of offering the interpretation more directly.

Then what? The counselor had wanted the wife to participate in counseling from the beginning, but she would not. The husband and counselor renewed the invitation with no success. As the client continued in counseling he strengthened in his ability to "hold the line" against her wheedling. With this situational success, he became more empathic, which helped him be patient with her.

3. *The saboteur wants to retain control.* The client is an adolescent female, seeking counseling because of recurring panic attacks.

Client: Mom wanted me to tell you that she thinks that I am not studying enough.

Counselor: What do you think?

Client: I'm doing fine in all my classes.

Counselor: What has she been saying?

Client: She thinks I shouldn't spend so much time reading the books you recommended. And she told me, loud and clear, that I don't have time to attend the assertiveness-training class you asked me to come to. She thinks I should go with her to a Bible study group instead.

Counselor: You're in a Bible study group now.

Client: Yes. But she says that if we are in the same one we can talk about what we are learning. And also, that I don't need the assertiveness class. She says, "You ought to just grow up naturally, not try to push yourself."

Counselor: How do you feel about your growing up?

Client: Like I'm way behind.

Counselor: She thinks you're up to speed; you think you're behind.

Client: Yeah. This is the way she likes it, I think. I even think that she is more comfortable with me trailing along behind.

Counselor: Say some more about that.

Client: She's always done a lot for me. She enjoys it. I am the big project of her life. I think maybe she doesn't want the project to get finished. Kind of like when you read a book and you enjoy it so much you wish it would just go on and on. You enjoy reading it so much you dread the last chapter.

Counselor: Being your mom has been enjoyable for her.

Client: Oh, yes! And she'd let me be a little girl forever if I would.

Counselor: But you don't want to stay a little girl.

Client: Sometimes I do. Sometimes I like it when she babies me. But I know it isn't good for me. I need to grow up; I know that. I want to. Most of the time, anyway.

Counselor: You've been working hard on that.

Client: Yes, I have. But she hasn't. She doesn't help me. She even gets in the way.

Counselor: How does she get in the way?

Client: She doesn't encourage me. Oh! Now I see! She encourages me in the things that keep me in the little-girl style. She sort of pulls me in the direction of the things she wants. I guess it's not that she wants anything bad for me, but that she just doesn't want to give up the kind of relationship we have had, because that has been so much fun for her.

Counselor: The book has been so good, she's dreading the last chapter.

Client: Yeah!

Counselor: You want to grow up; she doesn't want to give you up.

Client: Yeah.

Counselor: The decision you must make, then, is whether you will continue the process of growing up, even though that is hard for her to accept.

Client: Yes, that's it.

Comments: We knew that the client is overdependent in her relationship with her mother and that her mother fostered this. Now we are learning that her mother is so threatened by the progress the client is making that she is working against the counseling. We suspect that the saboteur's motivation is to keep her daughter, the client, dependent upon her.

The mother attended two consecutive sessions with her daughter. The counselor judged that, because of the mother's defenses, it would not be helpful to try to change her fostering of overdependence. The treatment goal was to help the client grow out from under the excessive nurturing in a way that honored the mother's role, yet led to maturity for the client.

4. *The saboteur wishes to maintain the status quo.* The client is a married woman, coming to counseling for help with a problem of jealousy.

Client: Honestly, there is no pleasing some people.

Counselor: Who's unhappy?

Client: (laughs) Me, for one. But that's not what I meant. It's my husband.

Counselor: What's up?

Client: He wanted me to get into counseling; now he wants me to stop.

Counselor: Has he explained why?

Client: He has his explanation for it; I have mine.

Counselor: I'd like to hear them both.

Client: Can I start with mine?

Counselor: Sure.

Client: Well, you know how much happier I have been since I've been getting over my jealousy.

Counselor: Yes.

Client: I think he liked me better the other way.

Counselor: What makes you think that?

Client: Since I quit that silly worrying about him, the stupid jealous worrying, life has been so much fun for me! I'm doing a lot more things, going places, meeting new people. Life is really getting interesting! But he's turning into a grouch. What do you think of that?

Counselor: I'd like to hear more about it.

Client: See, before, he wanted to go to lots of parties and places, and things like that. I didn't. Now it's the opposite. I enjoy going out and he's putting the brakes on.

Counselor: That must seem odd to you. How do you explain it?

Client: I can't say that I can explain it, but I have some ideas.

Counselor: Good.

Client: Here's my little theory. He *liked* my jealousy. It gave him a lot of attention. It made him feel important. Now the shoe is on the other foot. Before, when we went to a party, I thought I was going to lose him. Now, maybe he actually thinks he might lose me!

Comments: The saboteur seems to need control. Now that

his wife is becoming more, assertive, he fears that he will not be in control. He seeks to stop her personal growth by preventing her from coming to counseling.

From there? Oh happy day! The husband had been invited—no, had been requested—to take part in counseling at the beginning. He had declined. Now the counselor invited him again, and he came. The counselor spent several sessions building trust with the husband, getting to know him, affirming him, making it easy for the husband to speak from the heart. The husband, a scared little boy inside, grew up rapidly once he learned that he was no different from the rest of us.

There may be innumerable motives for sabotage and patterns of expression. Here are three more.

5. *The saboteur fears losing companionship if the client resolves his/her problem.* This saboteur is a person who feels inadequate—unworthy of the friendship of a healthy person. The saboteur's assumption is, "I'm not okay and if you're okay you won't like me anymore."

6. *The saboteur seeks to avoid counseling for self.* Knowing they need counseling, these saboteurs wish to discredit counseling as a means of excusing themselves from its discipline.

7. *The saboteur is angry and wishes to disrupt the client's life.* What greater pain might we inflict on people than to block them from the healing they need? This might be as an angry expression growing out of envy, in retaliation for hurt received from them, or as displacement of anger toward someone else.

LOOKING FOR SABOTAGE

As counseling progresses, the counselor observes the counselee's behavior and compares it with the goals of counseling. When progress slows or stops, the counselor looks for the causes, which may be within the person or in his or her "world." The counselor needs the individual's help with this, so he or she does everything possible to make it easy for the person to talk freely about everything of consequence in his or her life.

The counselor may suspect or discover sabotage from the person's friends or family members before the counselee does. If so, the best way to use such ideas is to guide the person toward discovery rather than describe the ideas directly. This is usually quicker, less disruptive, and more powerful than "spoon-feeding" the information.

Making interpretations about the person's friends or family members can be risky. Since your information about them is limited and second hand, the chance of error is great. He or she may have great loyalty to and affection for these persons (whom you view as saboteurs) and may rush to their defense. This will cause a disruption of the alliance between counselor and counselee.

In this segment from counseling with Elsa, a married woman seeking relief from perfectionistic traits, notice how the counselor leads her into discovery of her husband's attempt to sabotage counseling.

Elsa: I don't think I'll be able to come in every week because my husband needs my help at the store.

Counselor: Have you been working at the store the last few months?

Elsa: Only during the busy times.

Counselor: Is this a busy season for the store?

Elsa: (laughs) Oh, no! This is the *slowest* time of the year.

Counselor: The *slowest* time, yet your husband says he needs *so much* of your help that you won't have time for counseling.

Elsa: It's *his* idea for me to work there, not mine. He knows how important the counseling is to me, even though he hasn't had much work for me to do when I've been at the store.

Counselor: It sounds to me that *you* think he doesn't want you in counseling.

Elsa: I don't like thinking that, but, yes, I have been wondering just how sincere he is when he says he wants me to change.

At this point both the counselor and Elsa believe that Elsa's husband is trying to sabotage her counseling. They do not have a motive, although the counselor may have some ideas. Notice that the counselor led Elsa through a process of exploration and interpretation, a safe and productive approach.

WHAT TO DO WITH SABOTAGE WHEN YOU FIND IT

The counselor probably would like to verify whether Elsa's husband is trying to keep her from counseling. But how?

He or she could ask him to come in. If he is opposed to Elsa having counseling, would he come? It would seem not, but why not try? Elsa asked and her husband came; he didn't want to, but he did.

He came to counseling enough times to develop trust in the counselor and in the process. In time, the reason for his resistance to Elsa's progress was identified. Although not aware of it, he had feared that if Elsa became more relaxed and outgoing (as a result of letting go of her perfectionistic habits) she would become bored with him. They worked this through, and the marriage prospered.

That's a happy scenario. Let's consider one that is more complicated. Let us imagine that Elsa invited her husband to come in for a session and he roared, "No way! And I don't want you going back, either!" At the next session:

Elsa: Now what?

Counselor: You have a difficult decision to make whether to continue in counseling. If you do, you must be convinced that counseling is God's will as one of your actions of love for your marriage at this time. I think it is. You must pledge yourself to actions and attitudes that are good for both of you, and refuse to retaliate against him for his resistance.

Elsa: I'm not sure I can do all that.

Counselor: I'm sure you can, *if* you invite God's full partnership into this situation.

Elsa: Oh, I believe in that and I work on it as hard as I can!

Counselor: Yes, you *work* on it.

Elsa: Uh-oh! I forgot my lesson. *Work* isn't where it's at, is it?

Counselor: For you, not anymore! What is important for you?

Elsa: I need to rest, confidently, in the fact of God's love to me—to enjoy his *gift* of salvation. But, there will be some work involved in coming to counseling, won't there?

Counselor: Yes. It will stretch you. Even in that, however, part of it will be a discipline of *letting go*, not *doing*. To *not* be resentful about his anger, to *not* retaliate, to *not* allow fear to bind you. Basking in the certainty of God's love and sovereignty—accepting his love and forgiveness without trying to earn it by perfection—is an important part of that for you.

It is usually necessary for the counselee to take courageous actions in countering sabotage. The counselor prepared Elsa for that and provided support along the way. In situations of sabotage, the counselor will teach about the saboteur's motivations, help the individual develop compassion for the saboteur, teach assertive skills, and coach in applying them. These actions can bring tremendous challenge to the counselee: facing that saboteur assertively, fear of rejection, perhaps actual rejection or manipulative tricks in retaliation to the assertiveness. But facing these challenges can be gratifying and a leap forward in personal development.

Consider inviting family members into counseling. The same relationship of love that thawed the resistance of the counselee may warm the saboteurs to cooperation with healing processes. As they experience the gospel in and through you, they may recognize their sabotage, abandon it, and become allies. Does such massive change from a saboteur seem unlikely? Perhaps. But God advocates and supports reconciliation, so you can ask him to guide each of you into the changes that are needed. Follow his instructions, no matter how unlikely they might seem, and God will surprise you with his love!

PART II

RESOLVING ROOT PROBLEMS

THIS SECTION DESCRIBES PROCESSES of healing root problems. Each root problem will be illustrated with a case study of a person who has a disorder of self-control. In depicting the cases, some information about disorders will be presented, but the emphasis will be on identifying and healing the roots, just as it will be in your counseling.

The example in chapter 15 is more detailed than the others. It shows each of the seven stages in the Isaiah 6:10 sequence with particular attention to the root problem, a deficit of nurture from the counselee's parents.

The people you meet will be quite different from Bram or any of the other fictional characters in this book. You will, however, see in their lives many of the components and dynamics described in these illustrative cases.

CHAPTER THIRTEEN

SINFUL HUMAN NATURE: ERIC'S IMPULSIVENESS

THE YOUNG WOMAN'S VOICE WAVERED from exhaustion as she said, "He's done it again and I can't take it anymore." There was anger in her voice but it was blunted and listless, not sharp-edged as it had been before when she talked about the injustices being done against her and her children.

When the pastor had talked with Lisa earlier she had shown fierce hope that her marriage to Eric could become healthy. Today that fiery optimism was cold; she seemed worn out, defeated by Eric's repeated impulsiveness.

"What can I do? If he wants to trade cars he trades cars. If he wants to go on a trip we go on a trip. If he wants a new TV he gets a new TV. He's in his thirties but you'd never know it, because he does whatever he wants, whenever he wants to, just like a little kid."

PETER PAN IS ALIVE BUT NOT WELL

Eric's pattern is not a new disorder, but its prevalence has increased many fold during recent years of affluence and moral irresponsibility in American culture. It is described graphically by psychologist Dan Kiley in *The Peter Pan Syndrome: Men Who Have Never Grown Up*.[1] As Kiley reminds us, the fictional Peter Pan was a captivating youth who wanted to stay young forever. "I don't want to go to school and learn solemn things. No one is going to catch me and make me a man. I want always to be a little boy and to have fun."

In real life, adult-age Peter Pans can be captivating, too. They can be the life of the party: frivolous, prankish, entertaining, and spirited. They are a lot of fun, unless you need to depend upon them; they bring merriment and excitement, unless you are there on the day of reckoning; their parties are the best, unless you are the one cleaning up the mess.

In more technical terms they have the narcissistic personality disorder, which is characterized by grandiosity, expectation of favors and affection from others, lack of empathy and appreciation for others, and tendencies toward blatant manipulation and tantrums. In sum, these persons are madly in love with themselves. In America today the condition is not just a clinical syndrome but a distortion in the very fabric of culture, and the Christian community is contaminated by it.[2]

ERIC SAYS LIFE IS A TRAMPOLINE

Lisa persuaded Eric to come to counseling. The pastor, following good counseling form, tendered some small talk to build rapport and was amazed at the outcome. In Eric's self-centered world there was no distinction between small issues and large issues; there were only "me" issues and "them" issues. Trivia that interested him was of monumental importance, but an issue of substance such as world hunger would have been dismissed with a "let them eat cake" offhandedness.

When the pastor said "I understand you are interested in motorcycles" Eric leaped up and laid photographs of his bikes on the pastor's desk. When the pastor said "Lisa has expressed some strong concern about the future of your marriage" Eric replied, "She's always worried too much. She takes life seriously, which we all know can kill a person early, and that's dumb. Life ought to be good, don't you think, Reverend?"

The pastor nodded and started to speak but Eric continued.

"I knew you would agree with me. Life is a trampoline. If you put a little bounce into it you get a big bounce back and that's fun and that's what it's all about. Bounce, bounce, and have fun with it. The more you bounce the higher you go, up above the heads of the regular people, the ones who don't mind shuffling along their little path with their eyes on the ground, but that's not good enough for me! You wouldn't want me to shuffle when I can bounce, would you?"

Eric laughed and quickly added, with serious demeanor, "but I do need your help with something. I want you to teach Lisa that she ought to be bouncing with me better than she does."

Purposes and Origins of Impulsiveness

Self-gratifying behavior can be an end in itself—fun for the sake of fun. This approach to life is often the result of over-indulgence by loving but ill-informed parents. "The belief that a person deserves to have what he wants with or without asking is an archaic feeling from the past that will keep his life stunted and lifeless. The infantile fantasies that have never been resolved present major obstacles to the development of a healthy and positive relationship."[3] This leaves persons living at a relatively low level of development where most of the pleasures are sensate, and the more excellent pleasures that come from relational and spiritual development are unknown.

Exaggerated self-gratification may also serve as a defense against unpleasant conditions: to distract from fear, to assuage loneliness, to provide a sense of identity or meaning in life. This appeals to people who are low in confidence and encumbered with anxiety. Kiley's book attends skillfully to the problems associated with these conditions.

A third purpose of impulsive self-gratification is as a maneuver of defiance exercised by persons in spiritual rebellion. This was Eric's root condition. Let us understand his story a bit more completely, and then describe the general principles we may use to help people resolve that problem.

The Bondage of Eric's Freedom

The first time he had something repossessed by a finance company Eric took it in stride. "Who needs a motorcycle on a cold day like this anyway?" He walked directly to the used car lot with the huge yellow sign—KARL'S KARS, We Finance Everyone—and said, "Let's make a deal!"

The next time it wasn't as easy: the payments got steep and Lisa found out. It was hard to laugh it off when the telephone was disconnected, and the problems were piling up fast when his paycheck was garnisheed. So, he took Lisa out to dinner and told her not to worry about it.

She squelched her worry until she got so angry she threatened to leave. Then Eric said, "You don't love me. If you did you would be more fun to be with and if I don't have you I might as well end it all!"

So she talked with her pastor who, wisely, did not rush directly toward Eric but began looking for ways to get to know him. As that was proceeding, with some success, Lisa said things at home were getting worse, so the pastor asked Eric to drop by and see him.

During their conversation in his office the pastor could hear Eric's boisterous cheer echo in the emptiness of his life. As they talked the pastor prayed, *Lord, it seems to me that it is because Eric knows he needs you that he runs so frantically. Show me how to penetrate his prancing mind with the message of your love for him.*

Then the pastor said: You've told me a lot about what has been happening, and I appreciate getting to hear that. It would also be very interesting to me to hear about where you're headed. Want to tell me where you're taking your life?

Eric: People don't *take* their lives to places, they just *go.* Life gives you what life gives you.

Pastor: I want to understand that, so tell me some more.

Eric: We don't have any control.

Pastor: Would you like to have?

Eric: Yeah, but it just doesn't work that way.

Pastor: Can I disagree?

Eric: Sure.

Pastor: I think we have a lot of control—a lot of freedom.

Eric broke in: I didn't say we don't have *freedom*. I'm free as a bird. You get freedom by riding the breezes; you have to let them take you where they blow.

Pastor: Do you like the places the breezes take you?

Eric: A guy learns to adjust.

Pastor: Maybe I'm wrong about this, but from what you told me it sounded like some of your breezes lately have been tornadoes.

Eric: (chuckles) Yeah.

Pastor: If you could do something about that, would you?

Eric: If I could make the wind die down? Yeah, sometimes I think so, but, hey, something that scares me is when there isn't any wind at all. You know, those days when the air doesn't move—it just hangs there. On a day like that I feel like I'm going to choke. It's like the sky has died, everything so still like that, and—well, let's just say I don't like that.

Pastor: There's something about those super-quiet days that you don't like.

Eric: They make me nervous.

Pastor: You're more comfortable when things are happening.

Eric: Yeah.

Pastor: Some people are afraid of boredom. Maybe you're one of those.

Eric: Oh, wow! I never thought of it that way, but that's me!

Pastor: Then let me drop another idea alongside that one: maybe you keep bouncing on the trampoline because it gets scary when you're quiet. Maybe it seems to you that if you slowed down something bad would happen—you'd die or get captured and put into slavery—something would take away your freedom forever.

Eric: That would be the worst thing that could happen to me. It would be a waste of my life.

Pastor: And you don't want to waste your life.

Eric: No!

Pastor: What do you want to do with it?

Eric: Have fun.

Pastor: How's it going now?

Eric: I'm doing okay.

Pastor: You say "okay." Is that good enough?

Eric: No, but like I said, a guy takes what he gets.

Pastor: You're partly right. Everything you say is *partly* right. Wouldn't you rather be "righter" than partly?

Eric: I'd rather be happy than right.

Pastor: Happy comes after right.

Eric: How so? All these super-Christians I know who work so hard at being right are the most miserable people I know. It doesn't work for them.

The pastor thought of some theology lessons he could give but realized that it was more important to keep drawing Eric out.

Pastor: I guess looking at some of them turns you off, and I can understand that. Have you had some bad experiences with some Christians?

Eric: Christians don't have any fun.

Pastor: Guess what—you're *partly right*! (Eric smiled.) There *are* miserable Christians, which is too bad, because every person can have a better life with Christ than without Christ. Christ said "I have come that they may have life, and have it to the full." Some Christians are bored and grumpy because they haven't learned how to work the system.

Eric: Work the system? That sounds like street talk.

Pastor: You should learn more about the greatest street person of all time.

Eric: I hear you. You're talking Jesus.

Pastor: Sure, and he *can* be hard to trust. It was hard for me, anyway. I thought if I believed in him God would put me on a street corner playing a banjo, preaching, passing a hat, and starving to death for him. He doesn't pull stunts like that. He brings out the best in us. He lets me talk motorcycle with you but doesn't make me play the banjo.

Eric: (facetiously) Thanks!

Pastor: Yeah! And the point is, I can say "thanks" too, because God brings me into good things and makes my life larger and more interesting, not smaller and drab and painful. So it pays off for me to believe and obey, to "work the system."

126

Eric: Maybe that's easier for you to do because you're a preacher.

Pastor: Try it this way—I'm a preacher because it works, but it wasn't always easy and it's not always easy now. To start, I had to trust, and to do that I had to overcome some suspicions.

Eric: Yeah?

Pastor: I had been turned off to God by some people I saw.

Eric: Like you said, "I can understand that."

Pastor: You've had some bad experiences.

Eric: I had a Sunday school teacher cuss me out in class when I was a little kid. I've never forgotten that.

Pastor: Of course you haven't. What does it mean, now?

Eric: I'm pretty skeptical. Not about God—I believe in him—but I don't want him turning me into some kind of a looney-tune like that teacher, or into a monk or a missionary or something.

Pastor: You don't want your life to be wasted. You want your life to be enjoyable, to go to good places. And you figure that if you gave some control to God he would hold you hostage, just lock you up.

Eric: That's about it. I don't trust him.

Pastor: You ride a motorcycle very well.

Eric: Yeah.

Pastor: How well can you fly a 747?

Eric: Not at all.

Pastor: Sometimes we have more freedom letting someone else have control. For example, you have a lot more freedom letting a pilot fly you to Hawaii on a 747 than the freedom you have to ride your motorcycle to Hawaii.

Eric laughed: Yeah, I get your point. But since I don't trust the pilot. . . .

Pastor: You either don't go or you get acquainted with him and find out whether he can be trusted. One way to get acquainted is to talk to people who know him well; who have flown with him a lot. Like me. If you trust me, maybe you'll trust my friend. Do you trust me?

Eric: *Partly.* Except that you're trying to change me.

Pastor: I can see why it might seem that way to you, but I've got more sense than to try to change you because I know I can't. But you're *totally* right if you think I want you to choose some changes for yourself. What do you want to do?

Eric: I've got too many hassles in my life to make any changes.

Pastor: If you want to, we can talk about those hassles and maybe figure out how to straighten them out, and then we'll talk some more about hassle prevention—living with greater control and freedom. That's more than we can finish today, so let's decide when we can talk again—tomorrow if you want— so we can attack the pressures that are on you right now.

THE GOSPEL IN COUNSELING RELATIONSHIPS

The relationship of counselor to counselee imitates, with all the limitations of our human state, God's offering of mercy, grace, and wisdom to us. It would be blasphemous to make this comparison if God had not ordained it.

Because evangelism begins with the imitation of Christ, the pastor in our example determined to *be* the gospel before *talking* the gospel. He showed acceptance by things he did: listening, affirming, inquiring, clarifying. He built an atmosphere that made it easy for Eric to talk candidly; he earned the right to confront.

The things he did not do were also important. He did not condemn, scold, pontificate, or judge. He was concise in his references to his own experiences, did not rise to the defense of the inept Sunday school teacher, and used vernacular and metaphor in his own natural style.

Eric Finds Resolution of His Root Disorder

The pastor was the gospel in flesh for Eric in those conversations. As a result, Eric realized that his impulsive spending was his expression of rebellion against a God who would stifle him. The pastor was different—challenging Eric's assumptions and behavior, but affirming his personhood. Through this, Eric learned and believed the paradox that Jehovah God, who created us to be free, restores and expands our freedom when we give him control of our lives.

CONNECTING WITH REBELLIOUS PEOPLE

Persons in rebellion against God are usually suspicious of his representatives and must be approached with an extra measure of sensitivity. Several elements increase the prospect of helping them:

Prayer for wisdom. Let us ask for extra patience, discernment, and creativity.

Testimony of our life. The other person sees that we enjoy our lives.

Testimony in words. When we talk about our faith and Christian life we are concise, relevant, and appealing. The old show business adage about getting off the stage while they still want more is good advice.

Earning the right to challenge their behavior. Generally, we don't confront until we know them, and know them well. When we do, we confront the behavior, not the person. Better than doing that is to get them to confront their behavior themselves, which usually happens only after the appeal of Christ they see in us, and the truth of God's Word that we have helped deliver, penetrate their defenses.

Intercessory prayer. This is the most important item on our list because nothing we do will be constructive without the Holy Spirit's preparation. In fact, we risk damaging the other person unless God detains them and restrains us. This is where helping relationships should begin.

Summary

Persons in rebellion with God may develop disorders of self-control by repeating behavior which is done as a show of strength or to mask dissatisfaction. To help them, we must show the gospel before talking the gospel. This calls for abundant preparation (obedience in our own life, intercessory prayer, relationship with them that imitates Christ) before confrontation about disordered behavior.

CHAPTER FOURTEEN

PHYSIOLOGICAL INFLUENCES: CHUCK'S IDLENESS

"IF YOU THINK MY PROBLEM isn't a real one, look at this." Chuck pulled the right leg of his blue jeans up to midcalf to display his artificial limb. "Most of me is twenty-seven but this part of me is just a baby—eight months old."

He rapped on it with his knuckles. "It's made of the newest plastics and it's the deluxe model with the swivel ankle foot. I think I might get a radio put in it. Want to feel it?" He spoke with a smirk, as if begging me to reject him as he had rejected himself so many times.

Until he was in the eighth grade, Chuck thought the best part of life was playing Little League ball. It was what he did best until bone cancer led to amputation of his leg just below the knee, and suddenly it seemed to him that he couldn't do anything very well. His parents devoted themselves to helping him, doing everything for him except forcing him to help himself.

If he wanted something it was brought to him. If he wanted to go somewhere they took him. They carried him from the bed to the couch and back to bed for weeks that stretched into months, doing for him and doing for him. This was against the recommendations of their surgeon and physical therapists, but the parents blamed themselves for Chuck's illness and tried to work away their imagined guilt by catering to his every desire.

Chuck loved it and kept the system going. If his parents wavered in their efforts he pouted (warning one), shouted (warning two), or threw a tantrum (punishment). He trained them with his anger and created a serfdom of which he was lord and master.

Fourteen years later, he had a wife who wished she wasn't, two children who knew they were more mature than their father, an ulcer, and a powder keg of self-disgust. If he had any self-discipline at all he hid it under the chip on his shoulder. He sat on the couch two out of three months. Off and on he worked, a self-taught craftsman who had such uncommon skill that his employer (who was sick of his manipulations) could never resist hiring him back when he took a notion to work.

The first time I talked to him, in a formal intake interview, he said, "I'll tell you one thing for sure. If I come here for counseling I don't want counseling from you."

"It will be good for both of us if you tell me why," I replied.

"Because if you were my counselor you'd kick me in the rear and that's what I need, but it's not what I want."

I can't help wanting to counsel a person who knows what he needs and says what he thinks—the problems are out in the sunshine and that's the beginning of improvement! "You're right on all counts," I said. "Let's do it." And we did.

REMEDIES FOR THE ROOT PROBLEMS

Physiological influences need to be dealt with on at least two fronts. One, the counselor needs to push the disability aside as far as is possible. Every sensible avenue should be pursued and every reliable resource should be employed to minimize the extent to which life is diminished by the physiological condition. Christian counselors will be advocates for those whom they counsel, helping them make use of treatment and funding for services that reduce physical or mental distress and that enlarge the possibilities for living. Since Chuck benefited by having an artificial limb, it was right and proper for him to have the best one. (It didn't fit properly and he was afraid to be assertive with the supplier and the state agency who would be invoiced for the cost of adjustment. This became a counseling issue and a milestone of progress when Chuck took care of it.)

Secondly, we need to discern if the physiological condition is being used as an excuse not to develop in character or competence, "I can't go to work today because my leg hurts," Chuck would say. Or, "Would you run to the store for beer? My stomach hurts."

Chuck's Root Problem

Chuck had fixated at an immature level of development. Emotionally he was still a typical eighth-grader who liked to be gratified, *now!* This child of twenty-seven lived for his indulgences—beer and popcorn binges, watching TV, playing on his pool table in the living room, cheating at solitaire. He was the first kid on his block to have Video Pong.

His parents had unwittingly started the pattern and Chuck had quickly learned how to keep them maintaining it. He married young to Livvy who thrived on caring for him nine years, and then, almost overnight, was fed up with it.

Fun and games had not been enough for a long time. Even before Livvy's movement toward maturity (rebellion, he called it) he realized the shallowness of his simple pleasures and condemned himself for "wasting my life away doing nothing." He well knew the tug of war between sensate indulgence and growing up.

He was self-conscious about his slight limp. His self-condemnation exaggerated his self-consciousness. He felt, as people in shame usually do, that others were condemning him even more than he was. They didn't notice, of course. He finally broke the pattern when the saboteurs quit letting it work.

He wouldn't have done it without *them;* they couldn't have done it without *him.* Here's how it happened.

Livvy was on the verge of divorce, so Chuck, terrified, was eager to have her with us for two marital sessions to explore the possibilities. She preferred reconciliation, but was in despair about what to do. Bright, energetic, and ambitious, she was delighted with the person she was discovering herself to be. She was also genuinely in love with Chuck, and captivated by the realistic possibilities she saw for them. Uncommonly wise and motivated, she had to change first—and it took courage.

Chuck Decides to Grow Up

It was necessary for her to quit letting Chuck be a child—to refuse to play into his unhealthy dependence. The three of us discussed this. As Chuck gave verbal agreement he bristled with hostility as though he were covered with porcupine quills. We all knew a showdown was coming.

The issue was a summer trip with two other families. Chuck decided he wouldn't go "and none of the rest of you can either. I'm too sick to go. You have to stay and take care of me." They went without him. He had a tantrum Saturday and if they'd have been there he might have killed them. Sunday he had a hangover of such wretched proportions they might have killed him. When they came back Monday he had changed his mind about how he wanted to live.

"It finally got through my thick head," he said, "that I was being babied by my kids. I saw myself as a spoiled brat and them taking care of me, and it made me sick. How do I grow up?"

Slowly. People grow up slowly. There was no overnight transformation, but the turning point made all the difference—once he decided to quit hiding behind the leg that wasn't there he discovered strength in family, within himself, and, later, in relationship with Christ.

LESSONS FROM MULTIMODAL THERAPY

A system of treatment known as Multimodal Therapy has been developed by noted psychologist Arnold A. Lazarus.[1] This has been received with considerable enthusiasm by many

133

mental health professionals because it helps them design treatment to include strategies addressing each of the counselee's needs. Part of the counselor's function in this common-sense approach is to plan and oversee the helping process. Much of the work may be done by persons other than the primary counselor: medication by a physician, assertion training in a community group, or support in countering alcohol abuse in an A. A. group. Two things are accomplished: specialists do what they do best and all of the client's needs are attended to.

There are some lessons in this for Christian counselors. We can be *responsive* to each of a person's needs without asking of ourselves (foolishly) that we *provide* what is needed. We can serve as a creative director, helping the individual define needs and find sources of help, freeing us to do that portion for which we are best qualified. To do this we need to know the congregation and community. Churches contain many resources of healing, of which counseling is just one. It may be the most sensitive and expert arm for helping with serious problems, but it needs to work in concert with the others. Counseling does not compete with the others and it is no more nor less important.

Sources of support and growth within a mature (and I do not mean large) congregation include: worship, education, small groups for Bible study or fellowship, social organizations, the network of experts who can be tapped for such things as leads on employment, and the supportive services of deacons or similar groups. The Christian counselor in private practice, as well as those working on staff, should be able to direct hurting people to suitable sources of support and growth in other churches, Christian agencies, and in the city.

A MULTIMODAL RESPONSE TO WENDELL

Let's see how that worked out in counseling with a man named Wendell, and then consider the concept again in a more general way.

Wendell, age 47, had not been employed for seventeen years due to physical disability. His wife Beverly had taught school and was now self-employed. When they entered counseling they had just separated but both said they wanted reconciliation.

Wendell had needed, but never received, physical therapy and vocational counseling. The counselor helped him locate and enter state-funded programs for both. Apparently this brought hope that encouraged him because it was only after those programs started that he began to cooperate with individual and marital counseling.

Christian beliefs, both balanced and skewed, intertwined with the marital conflicts. The primary counselor helped sort out some of that, but Wendell always got a confirming opinion from another pastor before changing his mind. Good.

The family physician helped the man hold himself accountable and arranged for free use of facilities at a fitness club.

Due to the long period of intense relational and financial distress they had endured, resentments in the marriage were bitter. I cannot imagine resolution of those resentments without the confrontation and nurture of the Holy Spirit. Some of this came as they worshiped together; some through interdenominational Bible studies; some during private study and prayer. They became reconciled.

The multimodal approach involved two ministers, a physician, a professional counselor, a lay counselor, two community agencies, several Christian groups, family members, and friends. That seems like a lot of people, but it is fewer people than were being impacted while the couple was separated.

Inventory your church. List the resources of the church that can contribute to healing and growth in these areas: spiritual growth, vocational/financial, physical health, marriage, family, life skills, fellowship, and general. Then add programs and services offered to the community by other churches and community agencies you have confidence in. You will be delighted with the diversity and availability of modes of help you can access as part of your counseling response.

The resources of small churches are immense. When I was part of a church with two thousand four hundred members the list I made seemed impressive. Now I am part of a church with 5 percent as many members and I have made a new list, joyously discovering that the smaller congregation offers most of the growth-inducing opportunities of the larger congregation, plus several that are lost with size. There can't possibly be any correlation between the number of members and the potential as a healing community!

Summary

The influences exerted by accident, disease, and physiological anomalies of birth are real and they are powerful. They may be healed, but often must be coped with. They may be used to justify disorders of self-gratification. The corrective is to make strong, reasonable effort to help people reduce the destructive impact of the physiological condition and to deal firmly with the erroneous thinking that serves to justify the disordered behavior. A multimodal approach that capitalizes on all the resources of church and community to relieve, support, and strengthen is recommended. The resources of all churches are substantial; God's resources are unlimited. We are encouraged to think creatively and act boldly in faith.

CHAPTER FIFTEEN

DEFICITS: KEELY'S ADULTERY

KEELY DEVELENZA SIGHED AS SHE SAID, "I'm 38 years old and I've been married half my life. The married half has been the disappointing half. I expected a lot more from marriage than it has brought me, especially when I consider what I've given up for Nick."

I knew that she had a lovely home, two talented children, good health, plenty of money and leisure time, and that Nick remained boyishly in love with her. I wondered what she had given up and what was troubling her today.

"I want to understand how things are now and how you'd like things to be," I said. "That's a lot to talk about, so we'll just take it as it comes to you. Then, if you want to, we'll talk about what you can do to make things better."

She began by describing the many pleasant conditions in her life. I listened and occasionally paraphrased a bit of what she said to make sure I was understanding accurately and to show that I was listening. After about ten minutes of this she said, "All of these wonderful things, but I'm not satisfied."

"You're saying that something's missing," I replied. "Is it *just* that, or are there also things that *are* happening that are creating problems?"

"There is some of that, too."

"Then it will be important for you to talk about that, when you are ready."

She paused, exhaling slowly, and said, "Yes. I may as well tell you now as wait until later."

The next half-hour was intense. She alluded to a series of brief affairs in recent months and described feeling very guilty. "I have told God I am sorry and that I won't do it again, but I haven't felt any different. I have even been out with men since I prayed that, and I want to go out again. I think maybe God has given up on me."

I taught about God's relentless love for us, and Keely affirmed her repentance in prayer. I encouraged her to thank God for his forgiveness. She couldn't, so I did. Then, in the brief time remaining, I explained some things about the counseling process.

"You have done the most important things: confessing and repenting before God, committing yourself to learning a better way to live and to rebuilding your marriage, and beginning to trust someone who can help you. I commend you for all of that. Now let's talk about how you can manage your behavior during the next week."

Managing behavior. She decided to throw away some men's phone numbers she kept in her purse. This would not prevent her from calling, but symbolized her determination to change. She agreed to call me if she needed to. I wanted her to be accountable to someone other than me as soon as possible, but this was fine for the time being. I gave her a copy of Appendix 7, "How to Resist Temptation." She decided to ask Nick if she could be with him during at least part of a nine-day trip he was taking soon.

Fostering support. Keely was acquainted with several women I knew who had enthusiastic Christian faith. I asked Keely if I might ask one of them to invite her into a Bible study group they held. Keely liked the idea.

It was essential for Keely to know she had God's support. Given her experiences with men and her inability to thank God for his forgiveness, the approach to prayer needed to be easy and positive. "I want you to pray at least twice a day, but briefly and simply. Here's a pattern, 'Lord, I know you love me right now, the way I am. Thank you. Teach me the things I need to learn so my life can be better, as you want it to be because you love me. Thank you.' Don't get fancy; don't confess what God has already forgiven; relax in the knowledge that he is caring for you. In your own words, just say thank you for loving me and teach me what I need to learn."

Comments: After I knew the approximate dimensions of the disorder and saw Keely's commitment to change, there were two objectives for the session: (1) help her live effectively during the next week, and (2) begin gathering information that would lead to resolution of the root problems. Let's analyze this session in terms of the seven stages.

Stage 1: Manage the Crisis The DeVelenzas were in emotional turmoil but not in crisis; outside management was not needed.

Stage 2: See Keely had seen Christ in people and liked what she saw. We could reinforce that by connecting her with mature Christians. (It worked. The woman invited her out for lunch and Keely joined the study group.)

Stage 3: Hear She talked about the important matters and listened with an open mind.

Stage 4: Understand Keely disclosed the disorder in depth, but we haven't learned much about its origin.

Stage 5: Turn Keely showed that she wants (or at least will consider) "turning" by her choice of Christian counseling, receptivity to the Bible study, and agreement to control her behavior.

Stage 6: Be Healed Not an active stage yet, but Keely is doing things that will get her there.

Stage 7: Grow Participation in the Bible study will add knowledge, but this is not our primary emphasis now.

THE EARLY PART OF SESSION 2

Before Keely began counseling she had confessed her affairs to Nick and to God. Nick was belligerent for a month, then joined her in commitment to building a strong marriage.

She needed to understand and resolve the root causes that had led to her affairs. Let's listen in as that process begins.

1. Counselor: I am impressed with the way you have taken responsibility for your sins and how you and Nick have committed yourselves to building a strong marriage.

2. Keely: We both thought it would be easier to give up on the marriage, but deep down we knew how horrible that could be, so we decided to try to put it together.

3. Counselor: And the result?

4. Keely: It's a lot better already, and we have hope.

5. Counselor: Yes, you do! It's realistic hope because whenever you move in the direction God wants you to, you will benefit.

6. Keely: Nick and I believe that, so we're trying to be obedient. But it isn't easy. I still have a big problem controlling my thoughts.

7. Counselor: That can be difficult.

8. Keely: It is, and it is pretty scary to me sometimes.

9. Counselor: Please tell me some more about "scary."

10. Keely: Well, I get scared that we *will* give up; that I'll go back to an affair, or maybe even to having bunches of them. I guess that's my biggest fear.

11. Counselor: And there are some other fears?

12. Keely: I really don't know how to describe this, but I realize now that I'm spending a tremendous amount of time thinking about having an affair. Enough time that I don't get all the things done that I need to do.

13. Counselor: Even thinking about it, then, seems to be a problem to you.

14. Keely: Exactly! I worry that my thoughts will destroy me, even if I don't do the things I think about doing.

15. Counselor: Those thoughts are interfering with your life, but you don't know how to change them.

16. Keely: I want to.

17. Counselor: You can. Whatever God forbids you to do—and he does forbid lustful thinking—you can quit. You don't have to violate God's law. With his help you can reject thoughts you don't want.

18. Keely: Whew! What a relief!

19. Counselor: Let's talk about that some more before we finish today, but, in order to use our time well, let's do some more planning about what you want to accomplish during these individual sessions.

20. Keely: Okay, just so we are sure to talk about how I can push away those lustful thoughts.

21. Counselor: Yes, before you leave today I'll teach you several techniques to help you become free from those thought patterns. For now, can we put some more items on our "to-do list"?

22. Keely: Well, as you said last week, it is important for me to understand why I had the affairs and why they still look attractive to me.

23. Counselor: Yes. Good item. Now that you've had a week to think it over, are you ready to begin that process?

24. Keely: Yes, but I'm not sure I know how to do it.

25. Counselor: Part of my job is to guide you through the process.

26. Keely: I remember that you told me that some of it would be hard because it would probably take me back to painful things that have happened in my life.

27. Counselor: Often there is some pain—fear, grief, remorse—in the process of moving toward maturity. So, another one of my jobs as counselor is to support you through those difficult times and to pace the counseling so that there isn't more turmoil going on at any one time than is good for you. Fortunately, you and I aren't just in this by ourselves. We have other help.

28. Keely: What do you mean?

29. Counselor: Can you think of other sources of support that are available to you?

30. Keely: Oh! Of course! Nick is pulling for me. And praying for me. He put it on his appointment book to pray for me while we are in this session.

31. Counselor: Fantastic! That's terrific, to know that he is supportive right now. And, because he is praying. . . .

32. Keely: . . . God will help us. Sure! I'm praying for that.

33. Counselor: And I am too.

34. Keely: Still, it's going to be hard.

35. Counselor: So?

36. Keely: I don't care how hard it is. Because however hard it is to get better, I know from personal experience that it was a lot more difficult the other way.

37. Counselor: Good thinking. Things *are* going to get better because of your commitment, Nick's support, my help and support, and—by far the most important—the work of the Holy Spirit. Things are getting better already and, if you and Nick keep working toward a strong marriage, you will get one!

Comments: This excerpt from session 2 shows work in three stages. The numbers reference examples from the dialogue above.

Stage 2: See   The counselor continues to demonstrate reliability and competence (25, 27). Support is given by affirming Keely directly (1, 31, 33) and by enlisting support from Nick and God (37).

Stage 3: Hear   Keely describes what is going on (6–14). The counselor uses active listening (7, 13, 15) and clarifying (9, 11) as aids to accurate listening, and inserts some teaching along the way (5, 17).

Stage 5: Turn   Keely's continuing commitment shows (2, 16, 24, 36). The counselor will teach coping skills (19, 21).

The Latter Part of Session 2

Since Keely was motivated to change, we could move quickly into examination of her early childhood. She described it as "one long party." That was almost literally true. Her father, a gregarious and energetic sales manager, often entertained clients at home. Her earliest memories were of her parents asking her to stand on the coffee table to dance and sing for their guests. "I was Daddy's girl; I could do no wrong. I was an only child so he gave me everything he had. There was nothing like it—the fun we had together in those days.

"My mother was very pretty and pleasant; much quieter than my father but lavish in her praise. She didn't do as much for me as my father, probably because I lived for him. I would stand at the window for hours waiting for him to come home.

"One day he didn't. He was killed driving home from a trade show. I was thirteen at the time. Everything changed. My mother was never the same after that. She tried hard but she would get moody and quiet. She just got quieter and quieter as time went on and she never thought it was fair that Daddy died after she had worked so hard to make him happy and to help him be successful. I guess that's when my hard times began."

Keely was quiet and still. She looked at a blank spot on the wall across the room, but her eyes seemed to leave the room and travel back to her childhood town searching for her father; she seemed to leave the moment and travel back twenty-five years searching for his approval. "I miss him," she said quietly. "I miss him. . . . I miss him." It was a little girl's voice.

Comments: Keely is opening the hidden compartments of her emotions, a stage 4 process. In doing this she provides the material for understanding that will guide our quest for healing.

SESSIONS 3 THROUGH 8

"All I could think about this week was how much I have missed my father all these years. But even though I have missed him that much, I think I have never thought about missing him. Is that making any sense?"

It did. Her father was so important to her that she did two things: (1) pretended her sorrow was not as great as it was, and (2) looked for him in the form of another man.

Sessions 3 through 8 were given to stage 4 work. We gathered information to reconstruct the development of her disorder and identify the root problems. Here is how we organized our conclusions:

The Development of Keely's Disorder

Keely had two root problems: a deficit and a discrepancy. The more important of the two was the deficit of affection from her father, a problem that began before his death. The discrepancy—her mistaken beliefs about the role of a man in her life—exaggerated the consequences of the deficit.

The deficit. With the death of her father, her supply of emotional security and love from her parents was suddenly cut to less than half. Opportunities for attention from others and fulfillment of personal interests through social activities dropped sharply at the same time. Her need for harmony with other persons diminished. Her self-esteem, which had been precariously perched on her performances, crashed.

Discrepancies in beliefs. Keely had two erroneous beliefs that set her up for problems when her father died. First, she believed that another person could make her happy, just as (it mistakenly seemed to her) her father had made her happy. Second, she believed that if she were entertaining to other persons (as she had been at the family parties) that at least one of them would be responsive to her by making her happy (as her father had done).

These were the roots of her problems in adult life, believing that if she could generate merriment in the people around her, she was worthy. Within a few years of her father's death she discovered sex and the premium men ascribe to it as entertainment. She became very popular. This reinforced her belief that happiness and meaning could be earned by creating a party atmosphere.

Keely was attracted to Nick at first sight. His swashbuckling style was much like her father's. They fell in bed and thought they had fallen in love. They married. After two years and two babies, his compulsion to earn money (that had intrigued her at first) began to rule his life. Although he remained thoughtful and faithful, he was on sales calls most of the time. She didn't get much time with him; didn't "hear his applause" very often.

She was fearful about losing the man in her life (Nick) just as she had once before lost the man in her life (her father). Her level of emotional development was low; even her friends often described her as childish.

During the first counseling session she used the phrase "I'm good in bed" four times. She used sex in the marriage as she had before marriage: to get attention and an illusion of intimacy, and to escape conflict or loneliness. "We were like animals," she said. Neither she nor Nick knew how to resolve conflicts so when a disagreement started she would pull Nick to the bedroom. Because he, too, found solace in sexual expression, it seemed to work. Actually it only "swept the problems under the bed" and added to the discontent that would end in marital crisis.

Unfulfilled needs. She was sexually faithful to Nick, but other men, ogling her provocative dress and seductive mannerisms, thought she was available. She flirted subtly and she flirted boldly. Having practiced all her life, she was good at it. Nick didn't mind because he trusted her and he enjoyed seeing envy in other men's eyes. All she wanted was to be told she was worthwhile, but it prompted most men to fantasy and many of them to propositions, which she turned away. She just wanted to be wanted.

Nick, meanwhile, was being consumed by his ambition. They entertained business people lavishly in their home, much as her parents had during her childhood, but, although she and Nick were together a lot she began to feel more like a caterer than hostess and friend. When Nick became a district manager he was away from home three days a week. "I was lonely. Even on trips with him I didn't see him much and when we were together it was like I was a trophy of his success; it wasn't like being a person."

She had carried responsibilities as wife and mother with the emotional resources of entertainer and mistress. She had done remarkably well, but her marginal methods weren't good enough to cope with the next round of adjustments. Because she missed what she wanted most from Nick, assurance of her worth, it seemed to her that she had nothing from him.

Self-control disorder. When her mother died and the older

daughter left for college, Keely took the next proposition that a man offered. And the next. A six-month string of brief, half-hearted affairs reached crisis when she confessed to Nick.

Payoffs from the defective system of need fulfillment. The flirting, and to a lesser extent the affairs, assuaged her self-doubt and gave her what she thought was a sense of worth. The affairs temporarily relieved her loneliness and gave her an outlet, although improper, for her anger: part of her unresolved grief over her father's death and the loss of her mother, the emancipation of the daughter, and the erosion of companionship with Nick. She managed to gather a fleeting, shabby sense of control in this secret acting out against Nick.

Costs from the defective system of need-fulfillment. She was aware of her guilt and was ashamed. Nick saw to that. He made sure she was afraid of the future by threatening to divorce, to have retaliatory affairs, and to tell their daughters and other people about her affairs.

Then Nick changed his mind and said he wanted them to build a marriage and that he would do his part. There was one marital session (with Nick and Keely) between Keely's fourth and fifth individual sessions, but other marital sessions were deferred until more of her individual work was finished.

SESSIONS 9 THROUGH 11

Several important, though secondary, conditions were resolved during this period. Keely continued to understand and change discrepancies in her thinking, to affirm herself, to accept God's forgiveness with conscious enthusiasm, and to praise God with comfort and spontaneity. Counseling time was given to instruction and encouragement in these matters, and to preparation for a time of prayer for healing of the deficit of affection. Both of us were praying daily for God's guidance about it and in the eleventh session it seemed to both of us that the next session should be devoted to prayer for healing.

SESSION 12

This was scheduled for two hours so we would not feel pressured. Here are some excerpts from that session:

The counselor began with a summary and overview. "During

the weeks we have been meeting, we have regularly asked God to lead us toward healing of the parts of your life that have been broken or have not developed fully. We have been joined in those prayers by Nick and by several of your friends. We have been asking God to teach us how to pray and we believe that it is right for us to ask boldly today for the healing that you need.

"We have enough time that we can 'walk, not run,' in God's presence. As we pray we can be conversational—with God and with each other. We approach God with reverence and respect, but knowing his great love for us we can have confidence that allows us to ask questions and to listen to him. We can coach each other along the way if we want to. For example, if I am not praying for what is most important for you at the moment, you can simply say, 'Let's emphasize (whatever it is) now' and begin praying that way. Probably we will be silent part of the time, and that is fine.

"Let's begin by thanking God for his love for us and asking him to direct us in our time together."

The counselor and Keely both prayed. They praised God for his power and thanked him for his love. They celebrated the healing that had already been received and thanked God for the privilege of approaching him boldly with more requests.

"Teach us to pray, Lord," Keely asked, "because I want to be your person, fully alive for you—and for my family and me."

"Oops, is that all right to ask for?" she blurted in an aside to the counselor.

"Yes, and I join you in that prayer. Hear and answer this prayer, Lord of life, bringing the freedom and confidence that Keely asks for."

The praise merged into asking for discernment of God's wisdom. The counselor prayed, asking that Keely would understand whatever she needed to about the early parts of her life, and encouraged Keely to pray for that.

She began, "Dear heavenly . . . heavenly . . . dear . . . Lord, I wish. . . ." There was a long pause and she began again, "God, please teach me. I want to understand, heavenly . . . God, what. . . ." She sniffled and pinched her lips together, her eyes tightly shut like little fists.

The counselor said, "What are you feeling, Keely?"

"I better not say."

"It's okay to say."

"I don't think it's okay to feel this way."

"Feel what way?"

"Like I do now."

"What do you feel now?"

"I'm mad."

"That's okay. Who are you mad at?"

"That's what I don't want to say."

"Maybe you're mad at God, right now. That happens, and he understands that and if you are he wants you to go ahead and say so. Is that it?"

"Yes." The tears came, and sobbing—heaving, silent sobbing that had been hidden in a distant, inner place by Keely as a little child, when her pain was so great she didn't have words for it.

The counselor gently said, "This is part of your healing. Experience what is happening." He prayed silently.

Keely spoke softly in a pinched, child's voice. "I don't want to be mad. I don't want to."

"But you are, and it's okay. And you have been mad, Keely, and that's okay. God knows that, and God wants to tell you that he understands your anger and he loves you, and wants to take the anger from you. Will you let him tell you that himself and hand him your anger?"

Keely moved close to the desk, folded her arms on it, and bowed into her arms. Her choppy breathing subsided into a slow, steady rhythm.

"Bring Keely the healing she seeks. Answer the prayers we don't know how to pray, Heavenly Father."

Keely began to murmur in the little child voice, "Don't go, don't go. I want to show you what I can do. Stay and watch me. Don't go." The sobbing intensified.

"What's happening, Keely?"

"Daddy's leaving. Again. He was always leaving. A trip. Another trip. Always another trip."

"You wanted to show him something. What would you have shown him?"

"I was dancing. In my mind I see myself in a little tutu I had when I was about six, and I see me dancing in my room and he says good-bye from the living room and he leaves and I am in my room dancing and dancing and I just keep on dancing and I am crying—crying like I am now, and nobody is there to see me and I am so tired and I just keep on dancing. I can't stop. I know it is very late at night and I want to go to bed but I can't stop—I just keep on dancing."

"What do you want for this little girl?"

"I want her to be able to be at peace so she can go to sleep knowing that she is a worthwhile little girl."

"Can you let her do that?"

"I'll try."

The two had been silent for ten minutes when Keely raised her head. She looked relaxed.

"The strangest thing. In my mind I went in the room with that little girl, which of course was me, and I said to her that it would be all right if she went to bed. I explained that it was important for her daddy to take trips with his work and that he loved her just the way she was and that it wasn't necessary for her to show off for him to get him to love her. I said all that to her.

"Then the little girl crawled in bed and snuggled down, but then I was suddenly the little girl in the bed, and I heard a man say 'Let me tuck you in and say good night.' And he reached down and cozied the blanket around me and said, 'I love you just the way you are.' I felt all peaceful and I went to sleep with the greatest feeling of contentment, and knowing that things were okay.

"And then it was like I was moving back from the picture and I could see the whole room again, and it wasn't my daddy who tucked me in, it was Jesus, and he was sitting on the edge of the bed smiling at me and I could tell that he loved me."

She paused and, smiling, continued. "He *does*, doesn't he!" Her eyes were bright with joy tears, strong with confidence. "He loves me, doesn't he!"

Follow-up with Keely and Nick

This session was a turning point, but not the end, as is usually true with occasions of special progress. After this session

Keely made steady progress in eliminating discrepancies in her beliefs. Nick came with her to learn skills of marriage. They grew in Christian faith and practice, not without struggle and default, but with continuing commitment to one another and to their Lord and Savior, Jesus Christ.

Summary

What do we say about God's processes of healing life? We say too much, no doubt. *Everything is a variable except his love.* May we leave it at this:
1. Ask.
2. Believe.
3. He will.

The evidence: "I [Jesus] have come that they [you] might have life, and have it to the full" (John 10:10).

CHAPTER SIXTEEN

WOUNDS: CHERYL'S PERFECTIONISM

WE HAD BEEN TALKING TWENTY MINUTES in our first session. I said, "Cheryl, you mentioned that you are working in an accounting office. Please tell me some more about that."

She began crying. They were the largest tears I had ever seen and they ran freely down her cheeks and dripped onto her lap.

"I'm sorry. I don't want to be like this." She smiled, a wide and lovely smile that seemed to ask for reassurance.

Cheryl was an intelligent, attractive, Christian woman in her late twenties. In the interview she cried a lot but was creative in her responses, showed clever wit, and seemed motivated to work toward change. Her disorder of self-control was perfectionism. It is a disorder because it is not possible to control one's behavior perfectly. The perfectionist tries to, reaping certain frustration.

Her presenting complaints fit the clinical pattern called dysthymic disorder: mild depressive symptoms most of the time for more than two years, with feelings of inadequacy, pessimism, self-pity, and frequent tearfulness. The dysthymia was brought on by her failure to fulfill the demands she made upon herself.

Cheryl cried when I asked about her work because she had changed jobs four times in the last four months. The pattern had been the same each time: after two weeks she would begin calling in sick every other day, and she quit within the fourth week. She described intense fear of the men who had supervised her, and of other male executives in the companies. The day we talked she had skipped work two days on this job and was on the verge of quitting.

She had done brilliantly in college, had excellent recommendation letters (even from jobs she had terminated abruptly), and presented herself well in interviews. Each of her recent jobs carried considerable responsibility. She took work home from the office and continued to study accounting and read professional journals.

Her young marriage seemed stable and gratifying to both her and her husband. She described herself as a meticulous housekeeper.

Cheryl's parents were Christian and active in a strong church. The relationship with two brothers and two sisters was good. Given her reports of her fear of male supervisors it was natural to inquire about her father. He was unpredictable and occasionally explosive. He loved the children, but they were afraid of his outbursts which seemed to them to be unprovoked and, even in retrospect, uncorrelated with anything.

SEEKING THE SOURCE OF PERFECTIONISM

In our third session I was sure I should ask her to think back to situations in her childhood. We prayed, I aloud and she silently, asking the Holy Spirit to take her mind to whatever past events needed to be recalled and understood at this time. To reduce self-consciousness we turned our chairs away from one another. She closed her eyes and I was silent.

After three or four minutes she said she wanted to talk. Tears streamed down her face as she described an experience, something she believed she had not thought of since it had happened. Reliving it this day was, she said, as vivid as if it were happening all over again.

In this reexperiencing she was age eight, on her way home from school, skipping and singing with papers to show her parents, expecting them to be delighted with her good work. She entered the living room carefree and joyous. Her father came in and, without provocation, began scolding her in ugly fashion. Terrified, she ran down the hallway to her room, slamming the door behind her, throwing herself face down on her bed, sobbing uncontrollably.

We prayed again, asking God to bring full understanding of the situation and to heal the wound of that traumatic occasion. I asked Cheryl to let her mind take her through that again and told her that on this occasion Jesus would be present in the situation. Again, tears streamed down her cheeks, this time into the corners of her immense smile.

"Tell me what happened."

"It was like before, sort of. The feelings were so real it is like it just happened. It was the same thing: coming home happy and then my father yelling at me. I was so scared! I ran down the hall to my room and dashed in. I slammed the door behind me and I was going to jump on the bed as I did before, but Jesus was sitting on the edge of the bed, facing me. He held out his hands to me and he called me by name. He said, 'Cheryl, come here.' I climbed up on his lap and he put his arms around me and he said, 'Cheryl, it's all right. Your father doesn't know why he does what he does. Your father loves you, and I love you, and it's all right.' And he hugged me!"

With her eyes and cheeks sparkling with tears she smiled and said, "I guess it's all right." It seemed better than all right to me! Her eyes, which had darted in fear at the beginning of the session, showed peace and optimism.

I wasn't sure what it meant but I knew the Lord was at work. I prayed on behalf of us both, thanking God for bringing this experience to her.

Due to a trip, I did not see her for two weeks. I had asked her to continue praying for understanding and healing, but did not ask her to use the approach we had followed in the session. However, she did use that approach. On one occasion by herself she recalled another incident she believed she had not thought of since childhood. She was, again, about eight and her father was angry. Cheryl ran from him into a vacant lot behind the house. She ran until she dropped, exhausted. When her father caught up he took off his belt and whipped her.

In my office she told me, "I wanted to go through it again, asking Jesus to be there."

When she went through it the second time Jesus was there and she found herself on the ground, looking at Jesus' feet, thinking, "I'm safe. Jesus won't let my father whip me."

Father arrived, towering above her, and he took off his belt and whipped her.

"Then," she said, "Jesus knelt down, raised me up so he could hold me, and said 'Cheryl, it's all right, now.' I realize now that the history of the past can't be changed but the way we are affected by it can change. It *is* all right, now, that my father hurt me back then; it doesn't have to hurt me *now.*"

"How are things at work?" I asked.

"Fine! I like it!"

Summary of Cheryl's Disorder and Counseling

Cheryl had made impossible demands on herself, hoping that perfect performance would protect her from the disapproval and rejection she expected from other people. She had begun this pattern in response to the disapproval and rejection from her father, a man who seemed to cope with his displeasure with himself by criticizing and condemning the children. She tried to defend herself from his disapproval and rejection by being flawless at school and at home, believing that "they won't hurt me if I do everything perfectly." In return, she received a lot of approval for her performance. The system seemed to work, so she asked more from herself. But eventually it didn't work.

During her second reexperiencing of a whipping she forgave her father and recognized that his disapproval was due to his emotional problems, not to her inadequacy. Forgiving her father freed her of her fear of him and of men whose power reminded her of his power over her. She no longer needed to try to be perfect as a protection against criticism. She discovered that she had made demands on herself in her mind almost constantly and this habit faded gradually.

"When I became free to ignore my impossible demands, I began to realize how many there were and how impossible they were," she told me. "When I would start to whip myself with criticism I would catch that, and relax and compliment myself instead. And, I am sure that with the new attitude I am now able to do better than I had before when I was trying so much harder."

Cheryl was more effective on the job after she forgave her father. It liberated her from the bondage of perfection into the joy of excellence. When I talked with her two years after her "breakthrough" she had a better job in the same company where she was working the day we met, but was planning to quit soon because she was pregnant. She showed deep confidence in herself and said, "When other people in the office have problems they come talk to me because I'm the one who's got it together." She praised God for his grace and support.

Conditions Similar to Perfectionism

Regimentation is a way of defending against a fear of disorderliness or the unknown. The person believes *if I can manage everything around me it can't hurt me.* This simplifies life at first and may elicit rewards from those who benefit by the regimented person's structuring of things, but it is not possible for one person to bring order to a very large portion of a world that is disrupted by the chaos of sin.

Good works is another related pattern; it grows out of the fear of not living up to the expectations of a powerful person or of God and is based on the assumption that *I'll get rewarded if*

I do good things. Unhealthy excess in doing good is often aided and abetted by Christian culture.

COSTS OF COMPULSIVE STRIVING

Persons in any of these patterns feel a sense of failure, self-condemnation, fear of condemnation from others, and anxiety that they will not be able to keep up their efforts. They suspect that they are not functioning at their best.

They aren't. Research shows that those who strive compulsively for perfection achieve less than others and generate for themselves mood disorders and relational problems, just as Cheryl did.[1] When theology fails to teach grace the likelihood of perfectionistic striving increases.[2]

Counseling Cheryl was one of those remarkably exciting and joyful experiences in which the Holy Spirit led the process clearly and swiftly. It might be that if we were more receptive to the Spirit's direction this would be the norm, not the exception. For whatever reasons, counseling more often is lengthy and involves us in processes of searching the past, evaluating present attitudes and behaviors, weighing alternatives, and changing thoughts and behavior.

BREAKING THE CYCLE OF COMPULSIVE STRIVING

Disordered cycles of behavior are broken only after the person is convinced that the pattern is not working now and will never work adequately. Cheryl was convinced of that when she entered counseling, but often clients are not. So, we seek to help them discover that the payoffs of their disorder aren't worth the effort.

One method is to ask them to answer the question, "Should I attempt to be perfect?" During the interval between sessions they think about this fifteen minutes daily and write their answers: one column for advantages and rewards, and another for disadvantages and costs. Perfectionists, of course, develop detailed, long lists! Many have then decided that the benefits are not worth the efforts.

The mindset of the perfectionist has been shaped by a person of powerful influence, usually a parent. Again, beginning

as homework that is discussed in subsequent sessions, we identify that person. Inevitably we find that affection and approval
from that person were conditional upon performance, and we
will find deficits, wounds, or both. When these are healed, the
person is liberated from bondage. The remaining work involves
renewing the mind and adjusting to fewer harsh demands upon
oneself. This takes some time because the old habits will try to
assert themselves—but the client is enjoying a vastly improved
spirit while this is taking place.

RESOLVING THE ROOT PROBLEM OF WOUNDS

Forgiving and healing of the memories were the most important parts of Cheryl's recovery, just as they had been for Keely.
And the process again was a combination of strategies (which
we understood) and God's direct work (which was overwhelming in its power and would have seemed too good to be true
had it not endured). I interviewed Cheryl three years after her
"turnaround" and that tape recording resonates with confidence as she talks about the changes in her life.

She says, "I'm working two days a week now and loving every
minute of it. There are still frustrations, but they're no problem
anymore. If something happens that's my fault I can accept
that, but if it's not, I just let the others take care of it. I don't try
to take the blame for everything like I used to.

"I guess from my background I was taught that I had to do
everything right or God would punish me. And I was angry, I
realize now, with my parents—my father especially. You know,
he was never really a father to me at all. It was really a hard
thing for me to do, to forgive him, because he wasn't the father
that I needed. My friends had fathers, but he was never that
way.

"When I had trouble I would really feel angry at him because I would think, this is partly his fault because he didn't
teach me how to do things.

"Then when I was in counseling and I had those experiences
with Jesus being in those old situations I realized I wasn't to
blame for what my father was doing to me. Jesus was there
watching over it and he let it happen, but it wasn't because of

something I had done. When I realized that Jesus loved me and cared about what happened even if he didn't stop it, then I was able to forgive my father.

"Before, I couldn't do that because I thought God was so far away that he didn't care. Why should I forgive my father if God didn't care about me? The experiences enabled me to forgive my father for what he did to me. When I did forgive him, my life changed as much as from night to day and it's wonderful now!"

Wonderful showed all over her face!

FORGIVING AS A PROCESS OF HEALING

Wounds and deficits are injustices. Anger is a typical, if not inevitable, part of the human response to injustice. Anger, like a strong acid, is corrosive to our relationships with God and persons and to personal contentment. It is a symptom that has the power to create problems. Forgiving neutralizes anger. If we will, forgiving can flow over the anger and wash away the caustic before it eats holes in our happiness.

Forgiving does not happen in a moment, but *begins* at a moment of decision. It begins when the injured person chooses to let go of claims against the offending party: to relinquish the urge for retribution, to release resentment, to reject fantasies of the offender's painful demise.

In my counseling experience only a few things have seemed to be invariable. One of them is the intensity of the struggle to decide to forgive; another is the immensity of the rewards that follow forgiving.

Forgiving often seems impossible. Without God's help, it is.

Forgiving those who have been unjust to us—whether by sins of omission or commission—is contrary to our human nature which longs for justice, fair play, retribution, revenge. God calls us to what seems to be a higher standard, forgiving, which is an expression of mercy. To the mind of the world it is a higher standard, and an impossibly high one, but the obedient Christian discovers that forgiving is in our selfish best interest.

It seems that we must relearn this lesson every time we take offense at the actions of others. The wisdom we think we have neatly displayed on the coffee table in the reception room of our lives seems to evaporate in the heat of conflict. If we will see God and his remedies for injustice we will quickly be reminded of the importance of forgiving and of his readiness to support us in the process.

How to forgive? Do it. "I don't want to." Can you want to want to? "No." Can you pray to want to want to? "Yes, but. . . ." Do it. "But I don't want to pray to want to want to." Pray that you will be convicted. "But. . . ."

There is only one place to start: where you are, which is where God loves you now and where he will begin helping you do what you cannot do. It begins as soon as you say you're ready. Are you?

These are things I teach my clients who are hurting from injustices.[3] These, and my conviction that God wishes them freedom from the bondage of resentment. This conviction is a bedrock tenet in my life and it is delivered with vigor and persistence when it needs to be for two reasons: (1) because resentment brings death and forgiving brings life. This isn't overstatement; it is reality. And counseling itself is unjust if this message is not delivered when it is needed. (2) Because forgiving is intimate participation in God's grace, perhaps the ultimate human analog of God's mercy—a collaboration with God in which we are the hollow reed through which love flows—and it changes us even when we forgive but incompletely and momentarily.

HEALING OF MEMORIES

Is healing of memories a panacea for emotional distress? No. Is it a fad? Some places. Is it a legitimate expression of God's love and power? Yes.

It is also, for me, *mystery*: divine healing at work in ways I do not understand. It is *surprise*: the processes and outcomes have never been the same twice. It is *uncommon*: infrequently in my work I have been sure that this was God's direction for our counseling. It is *responsibility*: asking persons to open their dungeon of banished pain is not to be done carelessly. It is *joy*: when God has called me to accompany another person into that experience it has been a thrill beyond compare. To have the privilege of being with a person when

159

God resolves half a lifetime of anguish is certainly a gift given by him.

How is it done? That is a proper question but I urge you to be cautious of all answers to it except those that are cautiously given! Books by David Seamands[4] and H. Norman Wright[5] are good places to begin, along with books cited in chapter 10.

Several guidelines have earned a consensus among proponents of prayer for emotional healing.

1. God continues to give healing directly to individuals through extraordinary means.

2. A relationship of trust should be established first.

3. Learn about the personal background. Do not wallow in this, but from it identify the issues that need prayer.

4. Expect the person to do those things that are theirs to do through human channels: e.g., restitution, apologizing, confession.

5. Recognize that God heals life even when he does not heal a physical limitation such as a predisposition to biological depression.

6. It is desirable to have a small team of people praying instead of just one.

7. Take care not to dictate to God, which is unacceptable to him, but be free to ask boldly for him to do what is best in his way, in his timing.

8. Enjoy God's love.

Summary

God is in the repair business. He knows where the hurts are, so we ask him to direct us to them. He knows how they can be fixed, so we ask him to guide our processes. He knows how limited we are as healers, so we invite him to do the work. And he does!

CHAPTER SEVENTEEN

DISCREPANCIES: HOWIE'S PORNOGRAPHY

ARDITH DIDN'T RECOGNIZE THE VOICE of the woman on the phone. The woman said, "I don't know if you know it or not, but if you don't you ought to. Your husband is in and out of that dirty, so-called 'adult' bookstore like a regular customer. I wouldn't tell you, except for your own good."

Click! Ardith struggled to breathe. Dazed, she wandered around the kitchen, then into the bedroom. She sat on the edge of the bed, trembling and confused. Fearful of what she might find, yet hoping she might find nothing, she began searching the darker corners of Howie's closet. There, in a ratty old gym bag, was a collection of magazines showing people doing things she had never imagined.

Click! She heard the front door open and Howie's voice boom, "Hey, babe! Your man is home from the hunt!" She was panicky as she pushed clothes aside to put the bag back into the closet. She knocked a hanger of slacks to the floor with a crash. As she bent, terrified, to pick them up and put away the bag, Howie entered.

"What's up?"

His eyes dropped to the gym bag on the floor. Ardith slumped to the floor beside it, crying, her head numb with disbelief and fear.

Howie gave a tense laugh. "Oh, that stuff. I'd forgotten about that. A guy gave me that to keep for him. Uh, yeah. It was so long ago I forgot about it. At least three years ago. Yeah. That's the way it was."

He knew from Ardith's eyes that she didn't believe him. She struggled to force the truth that neither of them wanted, "Howie, one of those magazines has this month's date. I want to hear about it the way it *really* is."

Howie sat on the floor with his back against the wall, around the corner of the bed from Ardith. He drew his legs up, clutched with his arms, and slumped his head on his knees. He was silent for half an hour as Ardith wisely waited, quiet in prayer. Then Howie described his obsessive involvement with pornography. Ardith listened and did not pass judgment. She knew she did not need to; that Howie had condemned himself a thousand times. When she gave him encouragement to seek help for the problem, he said he would. He did not want to, but he knew he needed help.

SUMMARY OF HOWIE'S DISORDER AND COUNSELING

Lust is the relentless pursuit of any object. In Howie's case, the object was physical and emotional gratification through sexual fantasies. Counseling helped him find the root problems for his lack of control. The problem began with his mistaken belief that sexual performance is a mark of manhood.

Howie was a successful salesman for a sporting goods wholesaler. He was active in church leadership as long as he could work it in around sales trips and ball games. He and Ardith had been married for twenty-four years. "Happily married," they would quickly add.

Although sexual activity in the marriage was of typical frequency, neither of them was content with this part of the marriage. Ardith's enthusiasm for sex had been injured early in their marriage, they discovered during counseling.

Howie believed he was more of a man if he expressed himself sexually frequently. He sensed, correctly, that Ardith was somewhat put off by his aggressive, conquest mannerisms, but he was afraid to talk about it for fear it would turn a dull situation into conflict.

Instead, he began to fantasize about himself as the perfect lover, with a perfect partner, and began buying magazines to enhance the images in his mind. He failed to develop a sexual relationship Ardith was comfortable with and used her mild indifference to justify a form of sexual release that was less threatening to him because it did not involve emotional intimacy. This served to temporarily prop up his wobbly self-image.

Howie reshaped his thinking so he could rationalize his sin of pornography. His distorted thinking was, "I need lots of sex; Ardith doesn't. Since she won't provide what I need it is necessary to have another outlet. My choice of pornography is a good one because it doesn't hurt anyone." He had the problem; she got the blame.

This line of reasoning has some major flaws (e.g., pornography does not hurt anyone) and is built upon several false assumptions. Howie knows one of these (I *need* lots of sex) but does not know it is false. He is not consciously aware of some of his other beliefs, or that they are lies: (1) power equals worth, (2) sexual power is the most important kind of power, (3) a man is as worthwhile as his sexual performance. The credos weren't stated quite that way in locker-room parlance but he heard the messages over and over: "Only *real* men are worth anything and if you're a real man you're ready for sex all the time."

When Ardith showed Howie the gym bag we saw his shame and fear and learned that he had been struggling with his conscience for a long time. We saw Ardith respond with concern, control, and expectation for change. These were positives. He had been captive to the struggle for a long time, felt defeated, was willing to lie to cover his sins, and felt distant from Ardith. These were negatives. Through counseling the discrepancies that allowed Howie's disorder to grow and to continue were identified and corrected.

BREAKING THE CYCLE OF LUSTFUL THINKING

Breaking free from any disorder of self-control always begins with a choice that is based on information and energized by emotion. In most instances, constructive choices are made at times of crisis (hitting bottom) when emotion is high *and* when persons know a way out or have a guide they trust.

Counselors can teach individuals how to appeal to their own minds and emotions in the service of breaking the cycle. In all disorders of self-control, but perhaps particularly with lust (because it is private and pleasurable), it is necessary for the individual to take the initiative in breaking the cycle. Counselors cannot control what people think, but can give tools to help them control themselves.[1]

The Roots of Howie's Disorder

Christianity recognizes that sexual intimacy requires relational intimacy if it is to become a mature expression of love within marriage. Sexual perversions generally, and pornography especially, do not require relational intimacy or even relational comfort. Hence, they appeal to those who are not able to establish intimate nonsexual relationships with persons of the opposite sex.

The world says, "Kinky sex is the advanced course for persons who have mastered the basics. Adventurous persons who learn to fly an airplane in a straight line will get bored with that after a while, so they just naturally ought to go on and learn how to do aerobatic maneuvers." When you hear a person say that, question that person's ability to be relationally intimate.

The inability to form relational intimacy is often traced to deficits or wounds in the individual's relationship with the parent of the opposite sex.[2] That was true for Howie, and his counseling included attention to those issues. It is quite common to find more than one strand in the root system of a disorder, as was the case with Howie, but we describe here only counseling for resolution of discrepant beliefs.

The Principle of Displacement

Discrepancies come from thinking the wrong way. Paul warns about this: "See to it that no one takes you captive through hollow and deceptive philosophy, which depends on human tradition and the basic principles of this world rather than on Christ" (Col. 2:8). The corrective is to abandon the old way and begin a new way. Paul instructs about that with strong language. He says, "Put to death, therefore, whatever belongs to your earthly nature" (Col. 3:5) and "rid yourselves . . ." (v. 8).

He gives a system for doing this: displace the old with the new (Eph. 4:22–24; Col. 3:9, 10). Sometimes his language is general, "exchange the perishable for imperishable" (1 Cor. 15:53) and sometimes specific, "Get rid of all bitterness, rage and anger, brawling and slander, along with every form of malice. Be kind and compassionate to one another, forgiving each other, just as in Christ God forgave you" (Eph. 4:31, 32; see also 22–30).

Throw away the old and exchange it for new life in Christ, a process begun by faith and completed by grace, as we obediently seek to imitate the life of Christ.

We find the same method commended in the Old Testament. "Put away perversity from your mouth; keep corrupt talk far from your lips. Let your eyes look straight ahead, fix your gaze directly before you" (Prov. 4:24, 25). Stop, then do. "Take your evil deeds out of my sight! Stop doing wrong, learn to do right! Seek justice, encourage the oppressed. Defend the cause of the fatherless, plead the case of the widow" (Isa. 1:16, 17). Stop; do.

Helping Howie Resolve His Root Problem Discrepancies

The counselor worked carefully with Howie in early sessions, helping him manage his behavior. They used strategies described in appendixes 2, 3, 5, and 7.

The IDEAS diagram helped the counselor show Howie that his emotional distress had its source in erroneous beliefs. This diagram is shown in Table 6. The foundational discrepancy in Howie's thinking was that his beliefs about self-worth were in conflict with God's truth. The counselor showed Howie the flaws in his reasoning, taught God's truth, and gave him facts he could use to refute his bogus beliefs. Some of the approaches used in refuting Howie's damaging intellection were:

Howie at the Present Time

Intellection/Decision

2. sexual activity = worth
3. since I'm not active I'm not worthwhile
5. I would feel adequate if I were sexually active but sex with Ardith is not fun
6. that can't improve because we can't talk about it
7. I deserve whatever sexual happiness I can find
8. therefore, porn is okay
13. I'm no good and God is going to punish me

Emotion

4. inadequacy
10. physical pleasure
12. shame

God's Order

Enjoy sex with Ardith.
Porn is wrong. ◄——— **Conflict**
Be free from your guilt.

Situation

1.(a.) hears men brag about sex or
1.(b.) misperceives that Ardith is cool toward him
11. guilt

Action

9. spends time with porn

Table 6

Item 2, "sexual activity = worth." The counselor used the IDEAS diagram to show Howie why his present system was not working and to challenge him to demonstrate that it could work for anyone; to show how this assumption leads to conflict with God's order, and teach him where worth comes from.

Item 5, "sex with Ardith is not fun." This was challenged with questions that caused Howie to consider whether he actually believed what he was saying. Would you like it to become fun? Would Ardith? When has it been more fun? What is realistic to expect?

Item 6, "we can't talk about it." The counselor taught Howie communication skills; conducted a joint session to discuss the issues and demonstrate that they *could* discuss things; and pointed out that since he and Ardith apparently had talked constructively about Howie's disorder, could they not learn to talk about other difficult concerns?

Item 13, "I'm no good and God is going to punish me." The IDEAS diagram showed that it was Howie, not God, who was saying this. Scriptures about God's love and acceptance were presented.

The counselor helped Howie identify two situations, quite different, that triggered the chain of destructive events (Table 6, items 1a and 1b). Howie recognized that by being more assertive he could hear less sexual talk from other men and could understand Ardith more accurately. Disrupting the problem early would be helpful during the time he was receiving healing of the deficits and building his romance with Ardith.

A Way for Howie to Manage Situation 1(a)

Intellection/Decision	Emotion
2. that's not where it's at.	5. gratification
8. she loves me!	7. enjoy being affirmed
12. I'm okay and God loves me!	9. desire for sex
	11. physical pleasure

God's Order
Enjoy sex with Ardith.
Porn is wrong.
Be free from your guilt.

Situation	Action
1.(a.) hears men brag about sex	3. Pray "Thank you for Ardith"
6. positive response from Ardith	4. express love for Ardith nonsexually
	10. sex with Ardith

Table 7

Using the principle of displacement, the counselor did not stop after refuting the discrepancy, but offered replacement beliefs and behaviors that would bring the desired outcomes. The counselor showed Howie a sequence of logical thinking about his situation in another IDEAS diagram (Table 7). The counselor asked Howie if he preferred outcome 13 on Table 6 or outcome 12 on Table 7, and emphasized Howie's freedom to get the outcome he prefers.

Summary

Discrepancies are mental and behavioral conflicts between two people, between one individual and others, between the individual and society at large, or with truth, or conflicts within one's own system. The way to correct these is to displace untruth with truth and wrong behavior with good behavior. This method is described by Paul several times as a means of growing in Christian maturity. It is possible when people believe in Christ, which opens their eyes and hearts to truth.

The process can be guided by a counselor who can help make personal application and be an encourager, but human discernment and wisdom must be purified and augmented by the Holy Spirit. Most important, the counselee must have empowerment from the Holy Spirit in order to follow the new patterns. All of this is available to you and your counselees.

CHAPTER EIGHTEEN

RESULTS OF PERSONAL SIN:
NINA QUIT DRINKING, BUT . . .

NINA IS ONE OF MY FAVORITE PEOPLE. Everyone who knows Nina says that. We love her with a passion, but she's hard to explain, probably because she's such a wild combination:

She has the freshest look in her eyes you ever saw peering out of a weather-beaten face. You see the marks of twenty years of alcohol abuse and you see Christ's healing.

She is petite, moves gently, and seems timid, but you sense great power. If she were going to arm-wrestle King Kong you'd put your money on her and when she speaks you believe she could stop a stampede by shouting "Whoa!" She claws past nonsense and phoniness with the feistiness of a bobcat in a closet and when she listens to you, you feel your spirit massaged. She's different!

Described on paper she looks like she was constructed out of left-over parts that were fit together at random. When you know her in person you want to ask her, "How'd you get so wonderful?" and if you did you would hear the loudest, longest laugh you ever heard. Then she would give you an answer you would pray to remember word for word.

"Honey," she would say, "the Lord has been working on me a long time, and I gave him lots of time to think about it before I let him start!" She'd chuckle and continue. "Nobody recycles better than the Lord and I'm just proof of that, that's all. You can be too, if you want. We're all sow's ears, you know, but why not enjoy the status: we're the best creatures God made and he's shaping us toward perfection. Think of that!" She'd give her funny ladylike/childlike mini-whoop of delight, thrilled with anticipation of the person she is becoming—without pride or self-consciousness, just simple amazement at the glory of God's care.

Nina and I were in a booth at the quiet end of Barney's Cafe. "The last place in town where you can get a ten-cent cup of coffee," Nina said. "Where does he get off charging fifty cents for it?"

Then her eyes narrowed and wrinkles in her leathery brow converged as though pointing to her lips to call attention to something important she was about to say.

"I have a hangover."

Being surprised was one of the things I counted on when I talked with Nina, but this had me flat on the floor. I looked at her and thought about her fourteen years of sobriety and I looked at her again, trying to ask, but I couldn't manage more than "Wh—, wh—, wh—."

Then she took me out of my misery by saying, "When you're through whuffing I'll tell you about it, if you want to hear."

"Of course I do!"

"I've had a hangover for fourteen years and it's getting worse, not better. That's why I want to talk to you. I need your help." I felt like Einstein had asked me to help him with math.

"Uh, sure, Nina, but what makes you think *I* can help *you?*"

"You're my brother in the Lord's family, aren't you?"

"Well, yes, of course, but. . . ."

"Look! You let me be the judge of whose help I want to ask for, okay?"

"Okay. Sure."

"Now, about helping me, okay?"

"Okay."

Nina rubbed her lower lip between thumb and forefinger and frowned at the table top. "It's been nearly fifteen years since I took my last drink. But there's a lot that lingers on. Memories— a lot of things I know I'll never forget. How could I, with the pain to remind me?" She rubbed the back of her neck. "There isn't an hour of any day that I'm not reminded," she said, trailing off with a sigh.

Then she looked up, bright in the face and with energy, and said, "But I'm a conqueror! A child of God, sister to Jesus Christ, and going for glory!" She held her chin high and laughed, childlike and musical, deep from the heart, and turned studious again.

"You don't know this, because nobody but me and my doctor knows about this, but I'm telling you now and there is a reason why." She rubbed her jaw slowly. "When I quit drinking it was right after a bad auto accident. Most people who know me know about that but nobody knows what I am going to tell you now. I had—well, I still have—some nerve damage in the back of the neck. They couldn't do anything to really fix it. Surgery ran the risk of making things worse; physical therapy helped, but it was just temporary; and drugs, I wouldn't consider that. All it does is, it hurts. So, what was left was to live with the pain. Get used to it. Make friends with it. Get some good out of it.

"That's when I started learning about recycling. Pain is bad stuff—something to be gotten rid of—but if you can't get rid of it, then at least make something good out of it.

"Which is what I have tried to do. Every morning my first prayer is 'Lord, I don't want any pain today, but if this is what *you* want for me, bring it on, but I don't want it wasted. If this is what you want for me today, I only ask that somehow, someway, in your power and creativity bring value out of the pain. Do things your way in my life every minute of this day, whatever that takes.' That's my first prayer in the morning and my last prayer at night.

"Let me tell you what that has done. Before I told God the pain was okay, I wanted to die. I was hungry for the grave, believe me, and I thought a lot about how I could get there. But now I know that pain and God is more fun than the best buzz I ever got from a bottle or in any other way. You know what pain is? Hear about it from an expert—pain isn't when it hurts, pain is when you don't feel God. You know me. Am I happy?"

"You're happy."

"Yep! As a clam. As a bee in clover. Contented, at peace with myself and the world, and right now my neck feels like it's being sawed off but my heart is dancing a polka, my soul is kicking up its heels and shouting hallelujah. If this is sick, okay. If this is crazy, I'll keep it. If this is the way God wants me to live, it's the only way I want, too!"

With that she sat back, smiling, and we looked at each other for a long, long time. Then she leaned forward again.

"I think there might be people who are in the situation where I was years ago—they have a bad, bad problem that isn't going to go away and they're getting beat up by it. I wish I could convince them that God is in control, that he loves them more than they could imagine, and that their life can be good even if they have to endure a ton of pain or inconvenience or they are immobile, or whatever it is. I wish they knew that God created life and he keeps on creating life, and that even when the body is beat up the soul can keep growing and getting healthier and healthier. Isn't that wonderful!"

She leaned back, relaxed. "So, that's it! My hangover. What do you think?"

"You've blessed me again."

"Listen, don't think this is my last will and testament. I'm not planning on going anywhere right quick, but I was positive I should tell you about it. I want others to know that God heals life. Can we tell some people?"

"Let's put it in a book."

NOT EVERYTHING IS HEALED

God can heal everything but he doesn't. He didn't heal Nina's chronic pain. Why? Francis MacNutt lists fourteen reasons:

1. Lack of faith. (Matt. 17:14–20).
2. An individual's suffering can be of value, as Paul's "thorn in the flesh" was to him (2 Cor. 12:7) and his illness was to others (Gal. 4:13, 14).
3. The afflicted person does not want to give it up.
4. The suffering stems from unrepented sin, especially likely with the sin of resentment.
5. Prayer has not been specific enough.
6. Diagnosis is faulty, such as praying for physical healing when inner healing is needed, or praying in confession and repentance when the root cause has to do with the sins of others.
7. Refusal to use appropriate medical means as part of God's healing process.
8. Not using available means of preserving health, such as a person with emphysema continuing to smoke.
9. It is not the time.
10. A different person is to be the instrument of healing.
11. The social environment prevents healing from taking place.
12. Improvement is healing. For example, the cessation of pain, removal of side effects of treatment, stabilization of illness, or the return of physical function without healing of the illness all represent healing.
13. We must first stop sinning against ourselves.
14. The sickness results from evil in the larger community.[1]

This is a well-conceived and valuable list which I will modify only to *expand reason 5 to include not asking for enough.* No longer will I be reluctant to tell God all the desires of my heart, but will accept his invitation to "approach the throne of grace with confidence so that we may . . . find grace to help us in our time of need" (Heb. 4:16).

How Consequences of Sin May Lead to New Sin

It is not uncommon for consequences of sin to remain long after the sin has stopped and has been forgiven. Nina's chronic pain, the result of an accident while driving drunk, is an example. People suffer brain damage from drug abuse, liver damage from alcohol abuse, chronic or terminal diseases contracted during illicit sex, long-term or even irreversible financial loss, and similar consequences as the harvest of their sinful behavior.

Conditions like these diminish people's activity, bringing frustration which may generate despair about life and anger toward God. In rebellion new sins may flourish and a disorder of self-control may develop. In that situation, the consequence of former sin has been the seed from which new sins sprout. These developments are more likely when the person facing the problems feels powerless or unsupported, has discrepancies in thinking, or experiences shame. What are the options?

Helping People Who Feel Powerless or Unsupported

As we saw in chapter 14, collectively the church can mobilize extraordinary resources to support and motivate people. We can use the believers' network for healing instead of second-rate gossipy intrigue, to collaborate instead of compete, and to bring people together for mutual benefit. Churches can and should equip many people for relational ministries. Programs such as *How to Be a People Helper* by Collins,[2] *Servant Friends* (by the author[3]), and The Stephen Series[4] offer curricula and structure for this.

Helping People Who Have Discrepancies in Thinking

The most common discrepancy is an unrealistic expectation about the nature of healing. Nina was healed: not her nerve damage, but her life. During intense pain she testified to great joy.

How do we help people trade healing of body for healing of life? Let us learn from Alcoholics Anonymous and similar organizations which have demonstrated convincingly that people who have "been there" can gain audience in situations where others of us have no credibility or effectiveness. Churches have many "Ninas" with "I've been there" or "I am there" credentials. We can connect them with people who need their message.

When we have the level of trust and amount of information that permit effective confrontation, we may do more. We may puncture their excuses for hiding behind the difficulty (see chapter 14), teach about God's love and help them resolve anger toward God, help them hold themselves accountable (see Appendix 5.), and do the other things that are part of a loving attack on untruth. (See chapter 17.)

HELPING PEOPLE RESOLVE SHAME

The most common residual after sin has been forgiven is shame. It must be distinguished from guilt. Guilt is a condition of fact—estrangement from God that results from our disobedience. Shame is a self-evaluation—a highly subjective cluster of attitude and emotion that includes loathing and disgust toward self, embarrassment about self, and fear of being discovered as unworthy by others.

Guilt is corrected by confession and repentance, and *receiving* God's forgiveness. Shame is corrected by *accepting* God's forgiveness. This distinction has often been instrumental in the healing process. I explain it to clients in parable.

Imagine you had sent away to a mail-order company for a new jacket. After three weeks the United Parcel driver arrives with a package and you sign for it. You see the return address, the package is the right size and weight to contain the jacket you ordered—you know what you have received. Then you rush into the bedroom and bury the package, unopened, in the dark recesses of your closet. You have received the jacket, but it isn't doing you any good.

Accepting involves opening the package, shaking out the jacket, cutting the tags off, putting it on, wearing it, enjoying it, feeling good in it, getting the benefit from it.

We commonly hear about the need to forgive ourselves. The concept is right, but I prefer the phrase "accept God's forgiveness" to "forgive ourselves," which seems presumptuous.

How Jim Accepted God's Forgiveness

When my friend Jim was a child he was ridiculed and abused at school and in the neighborhood. In early adolescence he discovered alcohol and other drugs. That pretend world seemed better than his real one, so he stayed there for fifteen years even though it brought him twice to the brink of suicide.

When I first met Jim he had been a Christian for two years and had led three people to Christ. Jim knew that healing was far from complete in his own life, but he wanted to express his deep love for Christ by being useful to others. He entered counseling with Dale, a lay counselor, who came to me after three sessions saying, "Jim has some problems that scare me. I want to quit counseling him."

"Instead of that," I said, "let me join the two of you."

Jim was having surges of rage. During these times his hostility was so intense for a minute or two that he wasn't aware of anything else.

There was no question in Jim's mind that God had forgiven his sins. I asked him if he had ever thanked God for forgiving him and he had not; it was a new, appealing idea. In preparation, I described the distinction between receiving and accepting God's forgiveness.

We decided to thank God for Jim's salvation to make more tangible his acceptance of forgiveness that had been received. To help Jim, I prayed first, then the lay counselor, and then it was Jim's turn. Jim began, "Dear God, I have been a terrible sinner. Please forgive me for all my sins. . . ."

"Wait a minute, Jim. Haven't you already confessed and repented of your sins?"

"Yes."

"What was God's response?"

Jim thought for a moment, smiled, and said, "God forgave my sins. 'If we confess our sins, he is faithful and just and will forgive us our sins, and purify us from all unrighteousness' (1 John 1:9)."

"Then, Jim, since God has forgiven you and put your sins away, he doesn't want to hear about them again."

"Right!"

Our purpose clarified, we prayed again, and again Jim began confessing. We reviewed our theology and reaffirmed that this prayer was tangible expression of accepting God's forgiveness.

Jim tried, but didn't have any words. I asked Jim to say, "I am forgiven," but he couldn't. He tried again and couldn't.

He took a deep breath, pushed hard, and the words dribbled out, "I am forgiven." He said it louder and jumped to his feet with a shout, "Praise the Lord!" Dale jumped up with a booming "Hallelujah" and I popped up with a loud "Amen!" We hugged each other and praised the Lord for Jim's assurance of his salvation and his new sense of worthiness. Jim walked home late that night out of character—no, with new character—loudly singing "He's Alive."

The emotions were enjoyable but not important. Jim came alive. Gone was the backbreaking load of shame that squashed confidence and enjoyment, that inhibited friendship, and that kept self-criticism pelting his head like a hailstorm. Jim knew, that night, that his growth in Christian maturity was just beginning, but he knew Christ as his brother and that made all the difference. At this writing, Jim and I cocounsel with some other men, and what a joy that is!

Summary

Trash left over from old messes is a breeding ground for new messes. Some of this residual trash is removed by God's miraculous healing, some is recycled into strength of character and witness of God's ongoing grace, some is a nagging nuisance that brings a person to daily or moment-by-moment reliance on grace. When denied or misunderstood it is hazardous; when brought to the cross it becomes part of the process to shape that person more into the image of Christ, and that is the message of faith we wish to teach.

PART III

THE ONLY SUFFICIENT ANSWER

CHAPTER NINETEEN

CHRISTIAN MATURITY: WHEN?

THE ACHIEVEMENT OF MATURITY requires time, but time alone does not produce maturity.* Occasionally maturity outruns time, which may prompt the remark, "He is exceptionally mature for his age." Or maturity may lag behind, as when one scolds a teenager by asking, "Why don't you act your age?" Indeed, we may despair of maturity ever catching up with time, as when we say of an adult, "He will never grow up."

---

* This chapter was written by Orville S. Walters, M.D., a psychiatrist and ordained minister who understood the subject well and lived with uncommon Christian maturity. Written a few years before his death in 1975, and published as a leaflet by Light and Life Press, the material is reprinted here as a succinct description of the biblical and philosophical foundations of this book and as preparation for the next chapter.

The most obvious condition of maturity is the acquiring of knowledge. There is much one must learn before he can be called mature. In excusing the misadventures of a child, we may say, "He doesn't know any better." Most children learn rapidly. We hold them responsible—at least we should—in proportion to their knowledge. The learning process ought to continue throughout life, so maturing is really an ongoing process. Unless one keeps on learning, the process of maturing is likely to level off. This identifies the *intellectual* component of maturity.

But knowledge is not enough. We can all think of persons who do not exhibit maturity despite their learning. Profound learning does not necessarily prevent a person from carrying temper tantrums into adult life from childhood. Emotional arousal may sometimes overwhelm and supersede intellectual elements in the control of behavior, leading adults to behave like children. In the grip of fear or anger, persons may behave in ways that are later embarrassing, even though they "know better." Bringing the unruly emotions under control is an essential part of growing up. So maturity also has an *emotional* ingredient.

Even when knowledge and emotional control have been mastered, maturity may still be out of sight. The egocentric child may develop into a ruthlessly competitive, or even antisocial, adult.

A person may be emotionally stable and intellectually competent but if he violates the rules of courtesy and the rights of others, his ethical system is defective and he must be considered in some degree lacking in maturity. Hence *ethical* (as well as intellectual and emotional) development is a necessary condition of maturity.

BEYOND PSYCHOLOGY

Up to this point the conditions of maturity may be called psychological because psychology can throw much light on learning and emotional control. However, the recognition that there is an ethical component of maturity makes it necessary for psychology to acknowledge its incompetence and drop out. Since ethics asserts that one kind of conduct is better than another, an ultimate basis for comparison is implied. Ethical choices are basically theological since they imply loyalty to God or to some principle that stands in the place of God.

The intellectual and emotional components of maturity can be developed by effort, such as self-discipline, devotion to learning, and the cultivation of habit. Theological questions demand commitment. To live is to act, and to act one must make assumptions about the origin, meaning, and end of life. Every decision has ethical implications and is therefore in some sense a theological commitment, expressing the judgment that one value is better than another.

Believing that a proper ethic is one of the conditions of maturity requires a choice among competing ethical or theological systems. Many persons affirm their faith in naturalism. They believe that, in spite of present deficiencies, science will eventually have answers to all our questions about origin, destiny, and meaning. This view has wide acceptance in our time but is only an affirmation of faith. Another view places man rather than nature at the center, and makes a declaration of faith in his inborn capacity for self-improvement.

The Judeo-Christian faith asserts that both naturalism and humanism offer partial views of man. Contemporary Christians declare with Augustine that man is made for God and is restless until he finds rest in God. This faith, supported by a massive weight of evidence from every century, avows that relationship with God may be as real as with any human being.

Man may deny his need of God and rationalize his anxiety, but he cannot escape the overwhelming evidence for spiritual reality. Our "little systems" elevating nature or man may be brave, but they are shallow and inadequately based credos when competing with the mature Judeo-Christian doctrines of God and man.

RELATIONSHIP WITH GOD AS AN ESSENTIAL ELEMENT

If there is a transcendental component of reality, as Christian faith and a great weight of human testimony declare, then *spiritual awareness* must be included in any complete portrait of maturity. Sensitivity to divine reality is more than intellectual understanding. It is more than emotional stimulation, for the emotions may be subordinated and brought into subjection through commitment to God. Spiritual awareness is more than ethical choice, although profound ethical consequences may follow dedication to the Lordship of Christ.

Reality of the divine has proved throughout history to be an important aspect of existence. Thus, ability to perceive this reality must be included in the inventory of qualities that make up maturity. However well adjusted a person may be to his cultural milieu, he has a maturity deficit if he does not know or feel the reality of the divine.

The question, "Maturity: When?" is now partly answered. One is mature when certain intellectual, emotional, ethical, and spiritual conditions have been met. But personality is not divisible into parts. Since maturity is a property of the whole person, deficiency in any aspect bespeaks some degree of immaturity.

It is currently fashionable to talk about maturity. The layman, as well as the psychologist, pronounces rather freely upon the maturity of his fellows. Psychology may be entitled to generalize concerning knowledge and emotional stability as conditions of maturity, but it has no credentials for offering guidance in the less tangible areas of ethics and spiritual awareness. Those who have had a profound God-consciousness must also be consulted.

The apostle Paul had penetrating insight into the process of spiritual maturation. He recognized that various facets of personality must undergo development before one can claim to have reached maturity. Growth in knowledge is development in relation to our world. Growth in emotional control represents development in understanding and managing ourselves. Ethical growth requires development in our attitude toward other persons. Paul added to these the most important component of all, development in relationship to God, an ingredient often missing from contemporary definitions of maturity.

MATURITY AND PERFECTION

When Paul spoke of maturity he used the Greek word *teleios*, which signifies the final state of a progressive process. *Teleios* is sometimes translated "perfect," as when Jesus refers to the perfection of God in Matthew 5:48. "Be perfect, therefore, as your heavenly Father is perfect" can only describe an ultimate achievement, one never to be fully realized in this life. Paul recognized this in Philippians 3:12 when he wrote, "Not that I have already attained all this, or have already been made perfect, but I press on to take hold of that for which Christ Jesus took hold of me." *Teleios* is also translated "mature," as when Paul went on to indicate in Philippians 3:15, "All of us who are mature should take such a view of things."

The proximate *teleios*-maturity of Paul and the ultimate *teleios*-perfection of God both involve the possession of *agape*, the kind of love that comes from God. Paul identifies love as the most important ingredient of maturity when he writes, "over all these virtues put on *agape*, which binds them all together in perfect unity" (Col. 3:14). Love is the "bond of perfectness," the binder-together of all the qualities that make up maturity and that lead toward perfection.

This capacity to bestow unearned and undeserved love upon others finds little understanding in psychology. Freud pronounced the command to love one's neighbor as oneself "unpsychological" and "impossible to fulfill." He declared that nothing is so completely at variance with human nature. Freud, unacquainted with divine grace and unwilling to explore religion firsthand, generalized from his acquaintance with unregenerate man. He saw only one side.

There is a sense in which Freud's contention is true, that loving the unlovable is unpsychological. It is both contrary to man's natural inclination and beyond the reach of his unaided ability. But Paul knew something about man that Freud never learned—what divine love can accomplish in human personality. Describing the action of divine grace upon human nature, he wrote: "Once you were alienated from God and were enemies in your minds because of your evil behavior. But now he has reconciled you by Christ's physical body through death to present you holy in his sight, without blemish and free from accusation—if you continue in your faith, established and firm, not moved from the hope held out in the gospel" (Col. 1:21–23).

DIVINE AND HUMAN CONTRIBUTIONS

Reconciliation with God introduces man to the "more excellent way" of love and sets him on the long path to true maturity. The egocentricity of natural man gives way to the *agape* of God, which is "poured into our hearts by the Holy Spirit." Without this infusion of divine grace we can muster neither the inclination nor the ability to accomplish what Freud declared impossible.

As a complement to divine grace, Paul's imperatives imply that man is acutely responsible for his own development. He admonishes, "Put to death . . . what is earthly in you . . . immorality, impurity, passion, evil desire and covetousness. . . . Put them all away. . . . Put on . . . compassion, kindness, lowliness, meekness and patience." Then comes the ultimate ingredient of maturity: "Above all these put on love, which binds everything together in perfect harmony."

Is maturity a real destination? How much love is required? We open ourselves to divine *agape*. We add the full strength of our human effort. Still we find ourselves frustrated by inadequacy and failure to achieve *teleios*-perfection. The more saintly the person, it seems, the more sensitive he is to his own shortcomings, and the more modest his claim to holiness. When do we arrive?

There is no terminus in this life. The reach for maturity is a dynamic process that may continue as long as we live. *Teleios*-perfection is always in the future, for the destination is an ultimate one. But we should be more mature today than we were yesterday, and we should reach higher levels tomorrow as we grow in grace. In the lofty language of Paul, "And we, who with unveiled faces all reflect the Lord's glory, are being transformed into his likeness with ever-increasing glory, which comes from the Lord, who is the Spirit" (2 Cor. 3:18).

CHAPTER TWENTY

CHRISTIAN MATURITY: HOW?

THE COUNSELING PROCESSES IN THIS BOOK have assumed that humans have needs and seek to fulfill them. When needs are not fulfilled the deficits are real and can be quite painful. Persons often describe their condition literally: "in the hole" or "in the pits." This type of counseling is remedial: it recognizes the special needs and limited resources of persons "in the pits" and helps them get up to "ground zero."

We should not abandon them at that point, but help them move up or reach another plateau. It is appropriate for Christians to desire personal development in the realms of knowledge, emotional control, ethical conduct, and spiritual awareness and relationship. This type of counseling is growth-oriented: a gradual, life-long process that may begin with climbing out of the pit (stages 1 through 6 in our model) and walking the path to heights of joy (stage 7).

STAGE 7: GROW IN CHRISTIAN MATURITY

Pastors and other Christian counselors who are closely involved in a vital church can be extremely effective in helping counselees transition from remedial processes to growth processes. An active church offers many ways counselees can "connect" with worship and service, classes and workshops, and with people who can provide guidance and encouragement. Both counselor and counselee contribute to this. The counselee's part of the process continues throughout life.

Counselee Input

1. Manages behavior. The counselee continues to use what has already been taught: skills and attitudes that help control impulsiveness, ways to fight temptations (old and new), and disciplines that aid development of Christlike spirit and behavior. It is likely that the old disorder will continue to be the "Achilles' heel" or vulnerable temptation. Satan will continue to attack where he has had success before. Counselees should understand that temptation to an old sin does not indicate that they are weak.

2. Increases life skills. Counseling revealed the need for life skills that allow the individual to fulfill needs adequately at minimum cost. Learning should continue. The counselee may learn to listen more accurately and without judgment, and to communicate effectively. Vocational assessment, education, and improvement in job hunting skills may be needed. Group activities such as marriage enrichment and assertiveness training often are valuable.

3. Manages residual problems. The disorder may leave some permanent damage: e.g., a physical limitation, diminished vocational choices because the chance for education was squandered, or an angered family member who refuses overtures of reconciliation. Such circumstances can have gigantic influence and can seem overwhelming, but they need not preclude joy,

meaning, and contentment. God heals lives even when bodies or relationships are not healed.

Christians are commanded to be imitators of God (Eph. 5:1). Obedience to truth sets us free, in spite of the residual problems (John 8:31, 32)! For the Christian who is moving out of a disorder of self-control this is an opportunity to collaborate with the Holy Spirit and develop in love, joy, peace, patience, kindness, goodness, faithfulness, gentleness, and self-control (Gal. 5:22). These characteristics will make it possible, if the choice is made, to manage the chronic frustrations of a physical handicap or the heartache of rejection.

Counselor Process

1. Teaching. When counseling is Christ-centered and Bible-based, much information about Christian living is taught at natural points throughout the course of counseling. It is taught first (and most powerfully) by what the individual experiences in relationship with the counselor.

As the shift from remediation to growth occurs, the counselor becomes less actively involved, acting as guide and planner and helping persons hold themselves accountable. The resources of the church are introduced and become an important means of supporting the client (now former client) in knowing, worshiping, and serving Christ.

2. Discipleship toward Christian maturity. Counseling, especially when done by pastors, should be in the mainstream of church life. When it is, there can be easy and effective transition from counseling into worship, small groups, social activities, education, and other aspects of church life that are so important to each of us.

The counselor's contribution at this point is to help the counselee find the support systems that will nurture continuing growth: education, relationships, spiritual support, and opportunity for worship. This calls for knowing what organized activities are available and perhaps some phone calls to foster personal connections, but it may make the difference between lasting progress or relapse.

Christian living inevitably includes times of doubt, sorrow, and confusion. Counselees need to learn the norms of Christian living and understand how the annoyances and traumas of life can be managed.

I want counselees to know how salvation makes a difference in this life. It's a joy to teach about this and to be with people as they get to know the person of Christ. I teach that salvation marks a point at which:

a. We shift the emphasis of our life from destruction to completion.

b. We have the resources of the Holy Spirit for empowerment.

c. Healing of brokenness can take place to an extent not possible for the nonbeliever.

d. The Holy Spirit guides us into areas in which we need to grow.

e. We can have proper priorities (1) through the direction of the Holy Spirit, and (2) through Christian maturation (self-discipline, being part of a caring community, study of the Word, receiving teaching).

f. Our altruistic desires begin to grow.

g. We begin to be more aware of the needs of others.

h. We begin to understand the possibility of God working through us and begin to desire that he will.

Living in Christian community, receiving biblical teaching, practicing disciplines of study and prayer, enjoying fellowship with God, and being in worship lead to better judgment and more consistent living. As we mature as Christians, our perception of the nature of the world, self-understanding, and discernment in relationships become more accurate and more loving.

Illustration from Bram

The counselor had several sessions with Bram and Glenda to resolve some old wounds, and to teach communication and other marriage skills. Two sessions included the children. With the counselor's encouragement, Bram began meeting once a week with a small group of men for Bible study and prayer. Occasionally he would ask them for suggestions about how to manage a problem at work. Giving support and encouragement to others brought a new kind of satisfaction. Individual sessions tapered off to every other week, and then to a few monthly "tune-ups." After that, the teaching and support received at church made it possible for Bram to deal effectively with new problems as they came along.

Bram and his counselor knew that Bram dared not retreat to his former style of "clamming up" about his fears and frustrations. Bram pledged himself to talk quickly with Glenda about such issues and asked her to hold him accountable.

As Bram invested himself in study, prayer, and worship, his faith became meaningful and his relationship with God personal. As he put it, "Now that I know that I'm not in this by myself, I can fix the little things as they come along instead of letting them build up till I bust. It's sure a lot better!"

Hallelujah!

✿   ✿   ✿

Counseling requires love, courage, and compassion. Reading a counseling book requires self-control. I respect you for your commitment. On behalf of the people you are helping, and will help, *thank you.*

Of all the words in this book, these are the most important: "This is how God showed his love among us: He sent his one and only Son into the world that we might live through him" (1 John 4:9). May we know the one loving God better and better, and may we be creative and tenacious in sharing this greatest of all good news with others! May we live, *through him!*

APPENDIXES

SUMMARIES TO GIVE COUNSELEES

Appendix 1   How to Cope with Anger[1]

When the feeling of anger surges within you, the first step is to manage your behavior so you don't do something that makes the situation worse. This is "first aid." Then you can take steps to change the conditions within you and around you that lead to the anger. Use one or two of these methods to keep your behavior under control, but be sure to continue working toward a "cure" of the root causes. Some of them cannot be used in some situations you may be in, and some may not appeal to you. To be prepared, thoughtfully read the list now and circle five you think can be helpful to you. Keep those in mind so you'll have them ready when you need them.

Ask for God's help

1. Ask God to bring peace to your heart.
2. Pray for the person with whom you are angry.
3. Recognize that God is in control and thank him for that.
4. Pray with thanksgiving and praise for things that are going well in your life.
5. Remember or read Scripture.

Release physical tension

6. Take five deep breaths; release them slowly.

7. Listen to music you enjoy, play an instrument or sing.
8. Put your energy into a simple physical task (sweep the garage, mow the grass, take a walk).
9. Do something you enjoy.
10. Talk with a friend.
11. Talk with yourself eye-to-eye before a mirror.
12. Laugh.
13. Cry.
14. Write a description of what you are angry about, why you are angry, and what you plan to do about it.
15. Relax. *Control thoughts and behavior.*
16. Control yourself. You mentally "bite your tongue" and refuse to give freedom to your impulses. Do what you would do if a television crew started filming you while you are angry.
17. Measure the issue. Is it worth getting angry about?
18. Remind yourself that it is okay to have an angry feeling. Do not condemn yourself for your surge of anger.
19. Shift your attention to something else. Count to ten or recite the alphabet backward—thinking trivia is better than thinking hatred.
20. Separate yourself from the scene of tension if you can, if only for a few minutes.
21. Maintain positive thoughts. Replay your most relaxing vacation or your most contented moment.

Cautions

A. Avoid making judgments about people while angry.
B. Avoid making decisions while angry.
C. Don't drive.
D. Begin resolving the root causes right away.
E. Call your counselor if you need to.

Appendix 2 How to Stop Unwanted Thoughts[2]

This method applies Romans 12:21, "Do not let evil conquer you, but use good to defeat evil" (New English Bible). It has two steps.

Step 1

As soon as you have an unwanted thought, say "STOP!" Say it aloud if you can. Say it with energy and authority. Mean it!

This is helpful because it breaks the flow of the thought, punishes the unwanted thought, and is an assertive decision of your will to reject the thought. That's a turning point, but step 2 is necessary to complete the change.

Step 2

Immediately take your mind to an acceptable place. Think about something wholesome. Paul exhorts the Philippians to think about what is true, noble, right, pure, lovely, admirable—whatever is excellent or praiseworthy (Phil. 4:8). To apply this you might hum or sing a hymn, pray, read an inspirational article, recite a Bible verse, count your blessings, or give yourself a compliment.

If you can't do one of those things on the spur of the moment, start counting. Or, recite the alphabet (forward and then backward), count from 300 backward by 7s, or do anything else that puts your mind on something that is not destructive. It is better to think nonsense than to think evil.

Appendix 3 lists Bible verses on three themes. You might make a set of these on small cards to memorize, or to have handy as truth to displace unwanted thoughts.

This strategy works because, by choice, you displace what is harmful with what is good. Paul recommended this two-step process several times. When he instructs the Ephesians that "you must put off falsehood and speak truthfully" (4:25) and "he who has been stealing must steal no longer, but must work" (28) we hear step 1, *stop,* and step 2, *do.* His letter to the Colossians has a similar pattern of "stop, do" (see 3:1–17).

Although thoughts that have intruded for a long period of time usually do not disappear at once, many persons have found significant relief within two weeks. It is important for you to continue working on your other counseling issues during this time.

Appendix 3 Scriptures to Displace Unwanted Thoughts

Part of renewing the mind is to push unhealthy thoughts away by bringing in good thoughts. Nothing is better than the word of God! These Bible verses address specific needs. Choose a theme, look up the verses, and ask God to help you understand how they apply to you today. They will be even more helpful if you memorize them, or if you write them on small cards (perhaps one a day) to carry for quick reference.

God Comforts Fear	*Life Can Be Good!*	*God Has Forgiven Me!*
Isa. 26:3	Matt. 9:2	2 Cor. 5:21
John 14:27	Ps. 23:6	1 John 1:7
Matt. 11:28	Phil. 4:4	Matt. 1:21
John 8:36	Luke 6:23	Matt. 26:28
Rom. 8:15	Luke 15:23, 24	Acts 10:43
Ps. 23:4	Luke 15:7	Rom. 5:8
John 16:24	John 10:10	1 Pet. 1:18, 19
Phil. 4:6, 7	Ps. 47:1	Ps. 103:10, 11
1 John 4:18	Ps. 16:11	Titus 2:14
1 Pet. 5:7	Matt. 25:21	Rom. 5:9
Rom. 8:38, 39	Ezek. 34:26	1 John 1:9
Eph. 3:16–19	Neh. 8:10	John 1:29
Luke 12:22–26	Rom. 14:17	Isa. 53:5
Luke 4:18	John 15:11	Heb. 9:12
Prov. 4:25, 26	Ps. 112:1	1 John 2:1
2 Tim. 4:17	Rom. 8:6	1 Pet. 2:24
Isa. 43:18, 19	Luke 2:10	Acts 13:39
Isa. 41:10	Ps. 5:11	1 Cor. 6:11

Appendix 4   How to Break Habits

Recognize that breaking a habit is a process in which you learn new skills. Plan to change for a short period of time first, then for a longer period.

1. Ask God's help. Ask God to teach you the attraction this habit has for you, and to show you his alternative. Ask God to prompt you when you are careless in your own efforts and thank him for his assistance.

2. Hold yourself accountable to others. (See Appendix 5.)

3. Quit all at once. "Tapering off" rarely works.

4. Get rid of any objects of temptation or addiction (e.g., cigarettes, pornographic materials). If you keep a supply on hand you are not really planning to quit.

5. Keep track of your progress. Make a chart; put it where you and other people can see it.

6. Reward yourself for meeting goals.

7. Have a friendly, supportive competition with another person who is working on the same problem.

8. Be an encouragement to others with the same problem. The self-help groups that are successful in helping people break disorders of self-control invariably teach the importance of helping others.

9. Aside from the occasions when you are being a support to another person who is also conscientiously working on the problem, associate as little as possible with people who are giving in to the same problem.

10. Don't take a "do-or-die" approach to it, because that will increase your anxiety. Expect to relapse, but don't plan to. If you relapse, congratulate yourself for what you accomplished and begin again. Don't scold yourself for what you didn't do.

11. Rearrange your environment and schedule if you can. For example, a person who has lustful fantasies in bed after waking should get out of bed immediately and begin the morning chores instead of lying in bed.

12. Post supportive slogans and warning signs where you can see them. These might be as bold as a poster at home, or as private as a code that only you understand taped to your phone at work. For example, "NPO" (No Pigging Out!) or "TCFM" (Three Cheers For Me!).

13. Affirm your worth as a person. (See Appendix 6.)

14. Encourage yourself with positive thoughts.

15. When tempted to indulge in the habit, postpone indulgence for fifteen minutes. You are likely to be able to bargain postponement from yourself at moments when you are ready to give in. *Use the fifteen minutes to bolster your defenses against giving in!*

Appendix 5   Ways to Be Accountable for Your Actions

1. Set specific behavioral objectives for yourself. These must be expressed in such a way that you can measure whether you accomplish the objective. (For example, an objective "put 3 percent of paycheck into savings account" is measurable; "use money wisely" is not.

2. "Go public." Share your objectives with several persons whom you respect and who care about you. When other people know, you will get their support and encouragement, and it carries the threat that you will "lose face" if you fail.

3. Talk it up with yourself, too. The more often you hear yourself express confidence, the more likely you are to succeed.

4. Choose at least one special person whom you can phone any time you are close to losing control.

5. Promise one person whose opinion of you is very important to you that you will report any loss of control to them fully and immediately.

6. Include an unpleasant penalty for relapse: a fine, with the money going to a cause you dislike, or doing difficult household chores for someone else.[3]

7. Sign a contract about it, if that will help you accept the seriousness of being accountable. State your objectives and the terms of agreement between you. Each of you sign and keep a copy. Set a time limit between a week and a month. Renew if needed.

Appendix 6   Accepting God's View of Your Worth

It is right for you to think well of yourself. If you do not, your belief is different than God's belief about you. Wouldn't you rather agree with God? He is creating a wonderful person in your body! Be enthusiastic about that. The activities suggested here will help you think more accurately about your worth and become more free to enjoy the privileges of kinship with Christ.

1. Know the biblical basis for self-acceptance: We are created by God, given responsibility, and provided for (Gen. 1:28–31); God has special concern and purposes for each person (Ps. 139, Rom. 12:3–6). Although as sinners we are the opposite of God, he chose us and Jesus sacrificed for us (1 Pet. 2:9, 10; Rom. 5:6–8). Unconfessed sin brings distress but because God loves us he provides an alternative (Ps. 38).

2. Affirm in prayer the reality of God's love to you and thank him for it. You may wish to write such a prayer, or put it in the form of a thank-you letter to God.

3. Scripture assumes that love for ourselves is normal and desirable in repeating the injunction "love your neighbor as yourself" six times (Lev. 19:18, Matt. 22:37–39, Mark 12:31, Luke 10:27, Gal. 5:14, Rom. 13:9).

4. Ask God to teach you about every influence that reduces your enthusiasm for being the creature he has created. If this brings

awareness of the need to confess and repent, do so in gratitude of God's mercy and desire to shape you into a person more like his son Jesus.

5. If you have any doubt about the reality of God's forgiveness, tell him that in prayer. Learn the promises of Scripture (Appendix 3) about forgiveness. As you read a verse, pray, "Thank you, God, for _____" (summarize the promise of that verse).

6. Thank God for the fact of his *future* care over you. Celebrate the fact that life is meant to be good, with verses such as those in the "Life Can Be Good!" column in Appendix 3.

7. "Listen" to your "internal messages." Are you harsh with criticism of yourself? Be realistic; be kind. Keep high standards for yourself, yes, but be realistic and do not expect perfection. Use the technique in Appendix 2 if you need to.

8. Replace condemnation with affirmation.

9. Using a small list you can carry with you, write down things you admire about yourself.

10. Put on an advertising campaign on your own behalf. Each day for two weeks put up a small notice somewhere in your house that affirms you. Do not remove any of them until the end of two or more weeks. Put each new one in a different room each day. Do not remove them if anyone comes to visit. (Why shouldn't they know that you like you?) Say things like, "I respect you, (your name), because you discipline yourself for a daily quiet time." Or, "(Your name) is developing serious thoughts about growing in compassion for hurting people." Emphasize qualities of character as well as behavior.

11. Do this Bible study on Paul's attitude toward himself.[4] (a) See the balance in Paul's statements about himself (Eph. 3:8, 1 Cor. 15:9, 10, Phil. 3:13, 1 Tim. 1:12–14). (b) Note that Paul always gives God credit for what he accomplishes (1 Cor. 15:10; 2 Cor. 3:4, 5; 2 Cor. 4:7). (c) Yet Paul does not brush aside his considerable achievements (1 Cor. 15:10, Acts 20:27, 2 Tim. 4:7). (d) Paul is not reluctant to offer himself as an example of Christian faith in practice (1 Cor. 4:16, 1 Cor. 11:1, Phil. 3:17, 2 Thess. 3:7).

12. Read a book on self-esteem. Recommended books written from a Christian life view are:

Berry, Jo, *Can You Love Yourself?* (Ventura, Calif.: Regal Books, 1978).

Kinzer, Mark, *The Self-Image of a Christian: Humility and Self-Esteem* (Ann Arbor, Mich.: Servant Books, 1980).

Narramore, Bruce, *You're Someone Special* (Grand Rapids: Zondervan Publishing House, 1978).

Trobisch, Walter, *Love Yourself: Self-Acceptance and Depression* (Downers Grove, Ill.: InterVarsity Press, 1976).

Appendix 7   How to Resist Temptation[5]

1. Recommit yourself to Jesus Christ as Lord and Savior. Pray the ideas that are in this prayer: "Thank you, Jesus, for loving me enough to die for my sins. In the struggle of this moment, I reaffirm my belief in you and my determination to live in your grace in ways that please you."

2. Claim scriptural promises that victory over temptation is possible. See Rom. 8:37; 16:20; 1 Cor. 10:13; 15:58; 2 Cor. 12:9; Heb. 2:18; James 1:12; 4:7; 2 Pet. 2:9; 1 John 4:4. "Claim" means to hear them (read, read aloud, memorize) again and again with belief and thankfulness, so they become as deeply engrained in your being as your address. Then it is not just something you know, but part of someone you are.

3. Do not condemn yourself for being tempted. "Let no man think himself to be holy because he is not tempted, for the holiest and highest in life have the most temptations. How much higher the hill is, so much is the wind there greater; so, how much higher the life is, so much the stronger is the temptation of the enemy" (John Wycliffe). Christ was tempted (Matt. 4:1–11) and we will be too.

4. See the circumstances as part of God's life-building program for you. God, the Creator, can construct strength and beauty out of the rubble of your life—and he begins as soon as you want him to.

5. Ask for God's help. Ask for the characteristic that is opposite the temptation. For example, if tempted with sexual fantasy ask for purity in thought. Each temptation has a counterpart: stealing/trustworthiness, lying/honesty, selfishness/kindness, envy/love, infidelity/faithfulness. Ask! Ask early, urgently—but above all, ask with desire to receive.

6. Identify the high-risk conditions. In what places and at what times is temptation strongest? Keep track of this by making a few notes about it for a week. Ask God's help in this "detective work." When you know where and when risks are greatest you can counterattack. Avoid exposure. "Cross the street."

7. Don't toy with temptation. When you do, you are making a willful decision to prolong the temptation—siding with Satan in battering against the wall of your resistance. You won't win a battle of righteousness when you are on the side of evil.

8. Many coaches have said the best defense is a good offense. What are you doing to learn about God through study? How are you getting to know God personally through prayer and quiet time with him? What do you do in community with other believers to worship, fellowship, and serve? Get involved!

9. Learn to enjoy the "massage" of God's reassurance delivered through the Psalms. Ask God to teach and comfort you as you thoughtfully read and listen to God speak through Psalms 3–6, 10–18, 34, 40, 71, and 91.

10. Do things only if they are compatible with your beliefs, regardless of your mood. Satan promises immediate emotional payoffs that are never worth the cost. His highs are lies. If you act on the basis of God's truth, he can support your efforts and you ultimately will get greater emotional rewards than Satan knows about, including the best reward of all—joy and confidence in your personal relationship with God.

11. Thank God for the work he is doing in your life. He is already shaping you into his image (Col. 3:10, Heb. 10:14). Thank him.

12. Do all the wholesome things you enjoy with zest. Balance work and play.

13. Talk to yourself, aloud if possible. State what you will *not* do and *why* you will not. Spell out the costs of giving in to this temptation. Your private debate forces you to clarify your stand and reinforces your determination. Congratulate yourself for all the things you are doing well and for your moral strength.

14. Look ahead. "Pray that you will not fall into temptation," Jesus said (Luke 22:40). Regularly use the guidance of the Lord's Prayer, "lead us not into temptation" (Matt. 6:13).

15. Read Romans 8:28–39 and celebrate the fact that you are on the winning side! God, Creator of the universe, loves and protects you, now and forever, hallelujah!

BIBLIOGRAPHY

Backus, William, and Chapian, Marie. *Why Do I Do What I Don't Want to Do?* Minneapolis: Bethany House Publishers, 1984.

Beck, Aaron T. *Cognitive Therapy and the Emotional Disorders.* New York: International Universities Press, 1976.

Burns, David. *Feeling Good: The New Mood Therapy.* New York: William Morrow and Company, 1980.

Lawrence, Roy. *Christian Healing Rediscovered.* Downers Grove, Ill.: InterVarsity Press, 1980.

Meichenbaum, Donald. *Cognitive-Behavior Modification.* New York: Plenum Press, 1977.

Missildine, W. Hugh. *Your Inner Child of the Past.* New York: Simon and Schuster, 1963.

Rigdon, Robert M. *Discovering Yourself: The Key to Understanding Others.* Wheaton, Ill.: Tyndale House Publishers, 1982.

Scanlan, Michael. *Inner Healing: Ministering to the Human Spirit Through the Power of Prayer.* New York: Paulist Press, 1974.

Schmidt, Jerry A. *Do You Hear What You're Thinking?* Wheaton, Ill.: Victor Books, 1983.

Seamands, David A. *Healing for Damaged Emotions.* Wheaton, Ill.: Victor Books, 1981.

_____. *Putting Away Childish Things.* Wheaton, Ill.: Victor Books, 1982.

————. *Healing of Memories.* Wheaton, Ill.: Victor Books, 1985.

Stoop, David. *Self-Talk: Key to Personal Growth.* Old Tappan, N. J.: Fleming H. Revell, 1982.

Walters, Richard P. *Anger: Yours, Mine, and What to Do About It.* Grand Rapids: Zondervan Publishing House, 1981.

————. *Forgive and Be Free: Healing the Wounds of Past and Present.* Grand Rapids: Zondervan Publishing House, 1983.

————. *Jealousy, Envy, Lust: The Weeds of Greed.* Grand Rapids: Zondervan Publishing House, 1985.

Wright, H. Norman. *Making Peace With Your Past.* Old Tappan, N. J.: Fleming H. Revell, 1984.

NOTES

Chapter 3 The Beginnings of the Problem

1. Donald H. Ford and Hugh B. Urban, "Sigmund Freud's Psychoanalysis," *Systems of Psychotherapy: A Comparative Study* (New York: John Wiley and Sons, 1963), 109–178; Sigmund Freud, "A Philosophy of Life," *New Introductory Lectures on Psycho-Analysis* (London: The Hogarth Press, 1949), 202–233.

2. B. F. Skinner, *The Behavior of Organisms* (New York: Appleton-Century-Crofts, 1938).

3. John Dollard and Neal E. Miller, *Personality and Psychotherapy: An Analysis in Terms of Learning, Thinking, and Culture* (New York: McGraw-Hill, 1950).

4. Harry S. Sullivan, *The Interpersonal Theory of Psychiatry* (New York: Norton, 1953).

5. Karen Horney, *Neurosis and Human Growth* (New York: Norton, 1950).

6. Erich Fromm, *Escape From Freedom* (New York: Rinehart, 1941).

7. Eric Berne, "The Transactional Theory of Personality," *Principles of Group Treatment* (New York: Oxford University Press, 1966), 259–291.

8. Alfred Adler, *The Practice and Theory of Individual Psychology* (New York: Harcourt, Brace & World, 1927).

9. Abraham H. Maslow, *Toward a Psychology of Being*, 2d ed. (New York: Van Nostrand Reinhold Company, 1968).

10. Viktor E. Frankl, *Man's Search for Meaning: An Introduction to Logotherapy*, revised ed. (Boston: Beacon Press, 1962).

11. Carl R. Rogers, *Client-Centered Therapy: Its Current Practice, Implications, and Theory* (Boston: Houghton-Mifflin, 1951).

12. See: Conrad W. Baars and Anna A. Terruwe, *Healing the Unaffirmed: Recognizing Deprivation Neurosis* (New York: Alba House, 1976); Ashley Montagu, *Touch* (New York: Harper & Row, 1978).

13. Throughout this century there has been strong support for explaining human behavior and emotion as responses to needs. Some of the landmark literature is: C. L. Hull, *Principles of Behavior* (New York: Appleton-Century-Crofts, 1943); A. H. Maslow, *Motivation and Personality* (New York: Harper & Row, 1954); H. A. Murray, *Explorations in Personality* (New York: Oxford University Press, 1938). A personality theory written in lay terms and from a Christian perspective is: Robert M. Rigdon, *Discovering Yourself: The Key to Understanding Others* (Wheaton, Ill.: Tyndale House, 1982).

Chapter 5 Crisis Management in Disorders of Self-Control

1. This chapter gives an overview of management of crises that do not involve the threat of suicide. You are urged to read Judson J. Swihart and Gerald C. Richardson, *Counseling in Times of Crisis* (Waco, Tex.: Word, 1987) or other books referenced in this chapter.

2. *Newsweek*, October 23, 1972, 117.

3. For more detailed suggestions see: Charles P. Ewing, "Crisis Intervention: Helping Clients in Turmoil," *Innovations in Clinical Practice: A Source Book*, vol. 1, ed. Peter A. Keller and Lawrence G. Ritt, (Sarasota, Fla.: Professional Resource Exchange, 1982), 5–15; Eugene Kennedy, *Crisis Counseling* (New York: Continuum Publishing Corp., 1981); Barbara F. Okun, *Effective Helping: Interviewing and Counseling Techniques* (North Scituate, Mass.: Duxbury Press, 1976); Howard W. Stone, *Crisis Counseling* (Philadelphia: Fortress Press, 1976).

4. Judith A. Libow and David W. Doty, "An Evaluation of Empathic Listening in Telephone Counseling," *Journal of Counseling Psychology*, November 1976, 23: 332–337; Art Turock, "Effective Challenging Through Additive Empathy," *Personnel and Guidance Journal*, November 1978, 144–149.

5. Morton Bard and Joseph Zacker, "How Police Handle Explosive Squabbles," *Psychology Today*, November 1976.

Chapter 6 Counseling and the Problem: See, Hear

1. For suggestions about how churches can foster fellowship, see Donald L. Bubna, *Building People Through a Caring Sharing Fellowship* (Wheaton, Ill.: Tyndale House Publishers, 1982) or Charles A. Ver Straten, *How to Start Lay-Shepherding Ministries* (Grand Rapids: Baker Book House, 1983).
2. For more information about the importance of listening, and methods for effective listening, consult David Augsburger, *Caring Enough to Hear and Be Heard* (Ventura, Calif.: Regal Books, 1982); Thomas N. Hart, *The Art of Christian Listening* (New York: Paulist Press, 1980); Reuel L. Howe, *The Miracle of Dialogue* (New York: Seabury Press, 1963); or Richard P. Walters, *How to Be a Friend People Want to Be Friends With* (Ventura, Calif.: Regal Books, 1981).
3. The value of nondirective responding early in relationships is described in Robert R. Carkhuff and William A. Anthony, *The Skills of Helping* (Amherst, Mass.: Human Resource Development Press, 1979); Gerard Egan, *The Skilled Helper: Model, Skills, and Methods for Effective Helping*, 2d ed. (Monterey, Calif.: Brooks/Cole, 1982); Ralph L. Underwood, *Empathy and Confrontation in Pastoral Care* (Philadelphia: Fortress Press, 1985); Paul Welter, *How to Help a Friend* (Wheaton, Ill.: Tyndale House Publishers, 1978); and Everett L. Worthington, Jr., *When Someone Asks for Help* (Downers Grove, Ill.: InterVarsity Press, 1982).

Chapter 7 Counseling and the Problem: Understand

1. For more information see David A. Seamands, *Healing of Memories* (Wheaton, Ill.: Victor Books, 1985), 33–44, 145–147.
2. Paul Pruyser, a clinical psychologist in The Menninger Foundation, gives a strong plea for pastors to incorporate the distinctives of Christian faith in counseling in his book, *The Minister as Diagnostician* (Philadelphia: Westminster Press, 1976), 44–59.
3. For data on the influence of early development upon adult life see: W. Hugh Missildine, *Your Inner Child of the Past* (New York: Simon and Schuster, 1963).

Chapter 8 The IDEAS Diagram: An Aid to Understanding

1. Albert Ellis, *Humanistic Psychotherapy: The Rational-Emotive Approach* (New York: The Julian Press, Inc., 1973).

2. Lawrence J. Crabb, *Basic Principles of Biblical Counseling* (Grand Rapids: Zondervan Publishing House, 1975); *Effective Biblical Counseling* (Grand Rapids: Zondervan Publishing House, 1978).

3. William T. Kirwan, *Biblical Concepts for Christian Counseling* (Grand Rapids: Baker Book House, 1984).

4. William Backus, *Telling the Truth to Troubled People* (Minneapolis: Bethany House Publishers, 1985).

5. Everett L. Worthington, Jr., *How to Help the Hurting* (Downers Grove, Ill.: InterVarsity Press, 1985).

Chapter 9 Counseling and the Problem: Turn

1. Lawrence J. Crabb, *Basic Principles of Biblical Counseling* (Grand Rapids: Zondervan Publishing House, 1975), 98–106; William Glasser, *Reality Therapy* (New York: Harper & Row, 1965), 13–41.

2. Allen Fay, *Making Things Better by Making Them Worse* (New York: Hawthorn Books, 1978); William J. Knaus, *How to Get Out of a Rut* (Englewood Cliffs, N. J.: Prentice-Hall, 1982); Arnold Lazarus and Allen Fay, *I Can If I Want To* (New York: Warner Books, 1975); John M. Lembo, *Help Yourself* (Niles, Ill.: Argus Communications, 1974); Michael J. Mahoney, *Self-Change: Strategies for Solving Personal Problems* (New York: Norton, 1979); Richard Stiller, *Habits* (New York: Cornerstone, 1977); David Stoop, *Self-Talk: Key to Personal Growth* (Old Tappan, N. J.: Fleming H. Revell, 1982); Richard P. Walters, *Anger: Yours, Mine, and What to Do About It* (Grand Rapids: Zondervan Publishing House, 1981), and *Jealousy, Envy, Lust: The Weeds of Greed* (Grand Rapids: Zondervan Publishing House, 1985); David Wilkerson, *Have You Felt Like Giving Up Lately?* (Old Tappan, N. J.: Fleming H. Revell, 1980).

Chapter 10 Counseling and the Problem: Be Healed

1. I am thankful that the first books I read about divine healing were the two cited here, which are biblically sound and do not promote sensationalistic expectations. Each gives careful attention to why people may not be healed. See: Francis MacNutt, *Healing*

(Notre Dame, Ind.: Ave Maria Press, 1974), 248–261; *The Power to Heal* (Notre Dame, Ind.: Ave Maria Press, 1977), 57–61, 165–172.

2. In addition to books cited elsewhere, these have been inspirational and instructive: Theodore E. Dobson, *Inner Healing: God's Great Assurance* (New York: Paulist Press, 1978); Roy Lawrence, *Christian Healing Rediscovered* (Downers Grove, Ill.: InterVarsity Press, 1980); Michael Scanlan, *Inner Healing* (New York: Paulist Press, 1974); Dennis Linn and Matthew Linn, *Healing of Memories* (New York: Paulist Press, 1974).

Chapter 11 What To Do When Counseling Is Not Wanted

1. Robert J. Willis, "The Many Faces of the Hesitant Patient," *Psychotherapy and the Uncommitted Patient,* ed. Jerome A. Travers, (New York: The Haworth Press, 1984), 37–49.

2. Lawrence Tirnauer, "Problems of Commitment in the Psychotherapy Relationship," *Psychotherapy and the Uncommitted Patient,* ed. Jerome A. Travers, (New York: The Haworth Press, 1984), 27–36.

Chapter 13 Sinful Human Nature: Eric's Impulsiveness

1. Dan Kiley, *The Peter Pan Syndrome: Men Who Have Never Grown Up* (New York: Dodd, Mead and Company, 1983).

2. See Dan Denk, "I Wanna Hold My Hand," *His* (March 1982), 28–30; Henry Malcolm, *Generation of Narcissus* (Boston: Little, Brown and Company, 1971); Peter Marin, "The New Narcissism," *Harper's* (October 1975), 45–56; Eugene H. Peterson, "The Unselfing of America," *Christianity Today,* (April 5, 1985), 30–34; J. Isamu Yamamoto, "The Quest for Glory," *Spiritual Counterfeits Project Newsletter* (May-June 1984), 6ff.

3. H. Norman Wright, *Making Peace With Your Past* (Old Tappan, N. J.: Fleming H. Revell, 1984), 99. See also: W. Hugh Misseldine, *Your Inner Child of the Past* (New York: Simon and Schuster, 1963) 143, 144.

Chapter 14 Physiological Influences: Chuck's Idleness

1. Arnold A. Lazarus, *The Practice of Multimodal Therapy* (New York: McGraw-Hill, 1981); ed., *Casebook of Multimodal Therapy* (New York: The Guilford Press, 1985).

Chapter 16 Wounds: Cheryl's Perfectionism

1. David D. Burns, "The Perfectionist's Script for Self-Defeat," *Psychology Today,* November 1980, 34.

2. David A. Seamands, "Perfectionism: Fraught with Fruits of Self-Destruction," *Christianity Today,* April 10, 1981, 24–26.

3. See also: Richard P. Walters, *Forgive and Be Free: Healing the Wounds of Past and Present* (Grand Rapids: Zondervan Publishing House, 1983).

4. David A. Seamands, *Healing for Damaged Emotions* (Wheaton, Ill.: Victor Books, 1981); *Putting Away Childish Things* (Wheaton, Ill.: Victor Books, 1982); *Healing of Memories* (Wheaton, Ill.: Victor Books, 1985).

5. H. Norman Wright, *Making Peace With Your Past* (Old Tappan, N. J.: Fleming H. Revell, 1984); *Self-talk, Imagery, and Prayer in Counseling* (Waco, Tex.: Word Books, 1986).

Chapter 17 Discrepancies: Howie's Pornography

1. For more information on breaking away from sexual sin, see: Charles Mylander, *Running the Red Lights: Putting the Brakes on Sexual Temptation* (Ventura, Calif.: Regal Books, 1986); J. Allan Petersen, *The Myth of the Greener Grass* (Wheaton, Ill.: Tyndale House, 1983); Earl D. Wilson, *Sexual Sanity* (Downers Grove, Ill.: InterVarsity Press, 1984).

2. Leanne Payne, *Crisis in Masculinity* (Westchester, Ill.: Crossway Books, 1985).

Chapter 18 Results of Personal Sin: Nina Quit Drinking, But . . .

1. Francis MacNutt, *Healing* and *The Power to Heal.*

2. Gary R. Collins, *How to Be a People Helper* (Ventura, Calif.: Vision House, 1976).

3. Walters, *Servant Friends Resource Kit* (Ventura, Calif.: Gospel Light Publications, 1986).

4. Stephen Ministries, 1325 Boland, St. Louis, MO 63177.

Appendixes

1. Adapted from Walters, *Anger: Yours, Mine, and What to Do About It,* 65–73.

2. Adapted from Walters, *Jealousy*, 137–139. For more information see W. H. Cormier and L. S. Cormier, *Interviewing Strategies for Helpers: A Guide to Assessment, Treatment, and Evaluation* (Monterey, Calif.: Brooks/Cole Publishing Co., 1979), 339–347.

3. Items 6 and 7 are adapted from G. Alan Marlatt and Judity R. Gordon, *Relapse Prevention* (New York: Guilford Press, 1985), 257–259.

4. Based on concepts in A. A. Hoekema, "The Christian Self-Image: A Biblical and Theological Study." In W. L. Hiemstra, ed., *Proceedings of the 18th Annual Convention* (Grand Rapids: Christian Association for Psychological Studies, 1971), 8–21.

5. Some of this is adapted from Walters, *Jealousy*, 129–140. Another helpful reference was: Robert E. Speer, *How to Deal with Temptation* (New York: The International Committee of Young Men's Christian Associations, n.d.).

INDEX

Richard P. Walters, Ph.D.

Richard Walters is an author and counseling psychologist in private
practice in Boulder, Colorado. From 1982–1986 he was minister of
counseling in the First Presbyterian Church of Boulder, and from
1974–1982 he served as staff psychologist and director of the Life
Enrichment Center at Pine Rest Christian Hospital in Grand Rapids,
Michigan. He has conducted counseling seminars in North America
and Colombia, South America. His extensive writing includes articles
for professional journals, a textbook for educators, and several popular books, including *Forgive and Be Free; Healing the Wounds of Past
and Present.*

Dr. Walters graduated from Greenville (Ill.) College. He earned
the M.S. in business at Emporia (Kan.) State University and the M.A.
in counseling at Western Carolina University. He holds the Ph.D. in
counseling psychology from the University of Georgia.